WALKING
the MAINE COAST

2nd Edition, Revised and Expanded

Walking
the Maine Coast

32 Walking Tours
from Kittery to the
Canadian Border

by John Gibson

With Photographs by the Author
Maps by Lynda Mills & Glynis Berry

Down East Books ■ Camden, Maine

All directions, maps, and other materials in this volume were correct at the time of writing. Users of this book should use due caution in wooded or mountainous areas, as the reader is solely responsible for his or her own safety on these trails. Carrying a compass is suggested for the more remote walks in this book.

Copyright © 1991 by John Gibson
ISBN 0-89272-294-0
Library of Congress Catalog Card Number 90-84960

Cover Photo © 1991 by Rand Raabe (Monhegan Island)
Book Design by Lynn Ericson

Color separation by Four Colour Imports
Printed and bound at Capital City Press, Montpelier, Vt.

9 8 7 6 5 4 3 2 1

Down East Books
P.O. Box 679, Camden, Maine 04843

CONTENTS

INTRODUCTION

I have often thought, while poring over maps on a winter night, that there must be someone, somewhere, perched at a kitchen table at that very moment planning a visit to Maine. And that thought has led to another: Of all the people who come to visit this most fabled eastern state, how many will see the real thing?

Maine doesn't get into the news very often, but when it does it is usually because an intelligent soul like Charles Kuralt has managed to get an assignment editor to let him search for an America that has be-

come lost. When people grow weary with what rushed, urban America has become, they seem to think, inevitably, of Maine. And so, Americans edge a little closer to the television set or scan a magazine a bit more closely when the camera is turned toward the islands of Penobscot Bay, the stony hills of Acadia, or the northern lakes. Until the larger world becomes a lot more hospitable, this enthusiasm for Maine is likely to endure.

Much of the rest of America comes, then, to see whether some of the beauty, serenity, wildness, and scenic wealth that used to be so quintessentially American are still to be found. They come by car, by plane, by the busload, and even on foot or bicycle. (I had breakfast one morning with a young couple on Monhegan Island who were nearing the end of an eight-thousand-mile bicycle journey, and they were very glad to have discovered the Maine coast.) Many will only see the Maine that lines the few major travel arteries and the sights that any state with a tourist industry trots out for their delectation. But there is another Maine, the very one people hope to find when escaping from an overdeveloped, industrialized world elsewhere. For those interested in such things, this volume seeks to be their guide to some of the best walking ground in coastal Maine, otherwise known as "the real thing."

This second edition of *Walking the Maine Coast* contains specific directions to more than thirty invigorating walks in coastal villages, marsh preserves, shorelands, and seaside mountains. The walks range from easy strolls around villages famous for their unique attractiveness to more demanding excursions along the hilly trails of Acadia. Some of the routes described here offer the walker an up-close view of the bird populations and wildlife common at the coastline. Other walks take to the highlands, where opportunities for spectacular photography of major coastal headlands and islands will be found. As a whole, these walks are more or less evenly distributed along the Maine coast, from Kittery on the New Hampshire border to Moosehorn in the Calais area near the Canadian border. Included are walks in federal and private nature preserves, some of which are new to this edition.

To see a unique part of the world on foot is to change one's perception of it forever. It will come as no surprise that the author is partial to people who step out of their car, leaving the rush and hurry of the highway behind, and allow themselves time to experience the Maine shore, free of distraction. The natural world speaks to us only if we permit its restorative effect to grab hold. As I suggested to readers of the first edition of this book: Slow down a little. Put aside the rush that dominates too much of our lives. Experience intimately the positive, natural brand of America that Maine represents. This slowing down, this experiencing of Maine's coastline in an intentional, observant way, is a beneficial tonic. We begin to see things that we have missed for too long— good people; pleasant communities; the fascination of the shoreline, the hills, the woods— a natural world no less significant than our own, and from which we can learn.

Although most, visitor and resident alike, think of the Maine coast as a place for summering, there is no need to confine your coastal walking to just the warm months. Maine winters have a reputation for severity, but the coast tends to be milder than inland, and it is possible to make many of the walks in this book year-round. Routes in marshlands and in nature preserves just along the shore usually have little or no snow cover, due to the ocean's proximity, and make for good, brisk walking even in the coldest months. In fact, winter can be the *best* time for the marshland walks. In Acadia National Park, many of the trails and carriage roads can be walked, hiked, or cross-country skied right through the winter.

Unfortunately, it is no longer sufficient merely to enjoy the coast of Maine with no thought to its future. Unprecedented pressures for development and change now beset the coastal zone. The trails described in this book exist, in many cases, only because concerned citizens have fought to prevent the destruction of the coastal zone by runaway development. In short, the strange human penchant for digging up, commercializing, and thus destroying what we love is at work on the Maine coast, just as it is elsewhere. I suggest a challenge: For every hour you enjoy walking along the Maine shore, spend an hour working for its preservation, whether you are a resident or visitor. Unless all of us combat unsound destruction of marshlands, wooded shorelands, working waterfront, waterfowl habitat, intertidal zones, and coastal uplands, little will be left to enjoy in decades to follow. And we will all be the poorer for it. Contact the conservation organizations listed below and lend your hand to protecting the Maine coast.

Good Walking,
John Gibson

Maine Audubon Society
188 U.S. Route 1
Falmouth, Maine 04105
(207) 781-2330

Maine Coast Heritage Trust
167 Park Row
Brunswick, Maine 04011
(207) 729-7366

Sierra Club of New England
(includes Maine Chapter)
3 Joy Street
Boston, Massachusetts 02108
(617) 227-5339

Maine Appalachian Trail Club
Box 283
Augusta, Maine 04330

The Nature Conservancy
Box 338
122 Main Street
Topsham, Maine 04086
(207) 729-5181

Appalachian Mountain Club
5 Joy Street
Boston, Massachusetts 02108
(617) 523-0636

How To Use This Guide

This guidebook will direct you through a variety of walking and hiking experiences along Maine's border with the North Atlantic. Walks on islands, walks in small coastal towns, and walks in the woods are all included. So, too, are hikes up coastal mountains, along beaches, through marshes, and in historic areas.

EQUIPMENT. You don't need to be any kind of woods expert to enjoy walking the Maine coast, but some care in choosing footwear and clothing will add, surely, to your comfort and enjoyment.

Good walking shoes, preferably waterproof and rubber-soled, are appropriate for the "in-town" walks described in these pages. Lightweight boots, also waterproof, ensure your footing along the marsh, woodland, and mountain hikes.

Coastal Maine weather abides by few rules, changing almost without notice. For walks away from town, a sweater and lightweight rain jacket often prove useful. A compass, water bottle, and some lunch belong with you on the more lengthy or remote walks. All of these items will fit easily into the smallest backpack. Binoculars and a reliable camera can add to your experience of the outdoors.

MAPS. A small map, designed to provide enough information to orient you, accompanies each walk in this book. Should you get more ambitious in your coastal rambling, you may want to consult the maps of the U.S. Geological Survey. They are often available in hardware and sporting goods stores, as well as bookstores and stationers. Other useful maps of the Maine coast are available from Prentiss & Carlisle, 107 Court Street, Bangor, ME 04401. The Sagadahoc-Lincoln, Knox, Hancock, Waldo, Cumberland-York, and Washington county maps cover the coast. The *Maine Atlas and Gazetteer,* published by DeLorme Publishing Company, Freeport, ME 04032, is also up-to-date and helpful. For Mount Desert Island and the Camden Hills, Appalachian Mountain Club maps are available either in the AMC Maine guidebook or purchased separately. Order from the club at 5 Joy Street, Boston, MA 02108.

In most cases, unless you plan some off-route bushwhacking, the maps in this book are adequate without additional material.

When walking in areas where there are houses or private lands, please respect the privacy of the residents.

Walking in the intertidal zone may be slippery and sometimes hazardous. In fact, walkers should use caution while tramping anywhere in the woods or on the shoreline described in this volume. Use particular caution along the immediate shore when heavy seas are running, as unexpectedly high waves and strong undertows can sweep one off the rocks with little possibility of rescue.

Walkers will find additional routes for walking and hiking along the Maine coast in John Gibson's *50 Hikes in Southern Maine,* Backcountry Publications (Countryman Press), 1989, available in many bookstores in Maine.

WALKING
the MAINE COAST

1. Fort McClary & Fort Foster/ Kittery

When you are the "most" something, you attract attention. Kittery is that way, for it is Maine's *southernmost* community, and through it pass the majority of seasonal visitors to the Pine Tree State. The commercial side of Kittery along U.S. Route 1 is famous for its outlet malls and discount shopping places.

Kittery and Kittery Point display another sort of character, however, when you follow the north shore of the Piscataqua River out toward the ocean and discover the rural, historic, seagoing flavor of the towns. A walk that includes the old fortifications along Maine Route 103 from Kittery to Kittery Point and on to Gerrish Island exposes the tramper to some fine sea views, and lets one partake of the rich, historical flavor of the southern coast.

Kittery and Kittery Point "go back a ways," as locals put it. As Maine's first town, Kittery was organized in 1647. The Portsmouth Navy Yard (actually on Seaveys Island in Kittery) has been a part of the town's economic life since 1806. Many wooden ships that played an important role in America's infant navy were built on nearby Badgers Island in the late 1700s and early 1800s. The USS *Swordfish*, the first U.S. nuclear-powered vessel, slid down the ways at the Kittery Yard in 1956.

What better way to understand Kittery's importance as a coastal town than to explore her two old harborside forts, with a pleasant short walk between? To begin, drive east from Kittery center on Route 103 (Whipple Road). You'll pass many fine old homes and, after crossing Spruce Creek, spot the magnificent Lady Pepperrell House (1760) and the First Congregational Church (1730). They stand opposite each other at the sharp bend in the road.

The Lady Pepperrell House was once home to Mary Hirst Pepperrell (widow of Sir William) and was one of the most important Colonial residences north of Boston. Sir William Pepperrell, who was born in 1696 and grew up in a more modest house in Kittery Point, became an influential area merchant. In the mid-1750s, he was president of the Massachusetts Council and unofficial governor of the colony. In 1745, he led the expedition that captured the French garrison at Louisbourg in Cape Breton, Canada. Sir William seems to have been characteristic of that small band of Colonials whose deeds had a major impact on their time, as they functioned as soldiers, statesmen, and merchants.

Roughly one-quarter mile beyond these buildings, turn right at the Fort McClary Memorial sign. (Limited

parking is available here.) The walls of the old fort loom overhead as you approach. Some restorative work has been done, but the white, six-sided blockhouse is the only portion of the fort reflecting recent repair. One doesn't need to be a military buff to enjoy scrambling over the grass-covered fortifications that look across Portsmouth Harbor toward Newcastle.

These fortifications date from 1690, when some sort of defensible community refuge from Indian attacks was necessary. First known as Pepperrell's Fort and later as Fort William, the post was subsequently named after Major Andrew McClary, fallen Bunker Hill patriot. Standing on the battlements and looking back to the land or out toward the sea, you will understand at once why this particular point was fortified; a more advantageous location from which to repel either land or sea attacks would be hard to imagine.

To reach Fort Foster, leave your car here or in the parking area across the road, where a picnic area for visitors has been created diagonally opposite the entrance to Fort McClary. (There are picnic benches, grills, swings, and room to park well off the road in a pleasant, pine-studded setting.) Now walk east on Pepperrell Road, watching carefully for traffic, which is often heavy in summer. In four-tenths of a mile, you come to Frisbee's Market, the oldest family-run store in America. Down behind the store are the town docks, alive with boating activity during the warmer months and very much worth visiting. In another half-mile, bear right on Chaunceys Creek Road. This pleasant country road follows the creek eastward, with some fine outlooks back to the southwest and

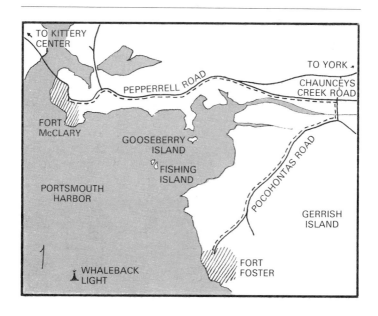

toward the harbor. You will soon turn right at the intersection and cross the bridge to Gerrish Island. The scene here typifies coastal Maine: small, snug Capes hug the hillside, evergreens blanket the island shore, and lobster gear sits stacked on the weathered docks below, waiting to be borne outward by the boats moored nearby.

Across the bridge and on the island, you bear right and walk south on a paved way known as Pocohontas Road. The walk here lies through pretty, forested land with few houses. In 1.2 miles you bear right at a fork and come to the entrance of Fort Foster Reservation (a small entrance fee may be charged in high summer).

Construction of Fort Foster began shortly after the Civil War, and the facility remained active until after World War II. The post takes its name from Major General John Foster, a New Hampshire native who distinguished himself in the Mexican wars. The battlements, like those at Fort McClary, lend themselves to some interesting exploration. Other attractive walks around the area via side roads and paths are marked by signs near the main gate.

The most appealing views are certainly those across the broad channel toward New Hampshire. More to the left, if the weather is clear, you'll see a small cluster of islands on the horizon. These are the fabled Isles of Shoals. Most prominent is the lighthouse on White Island. Closer at hand, you will spot Whaleback Light on the ledges at the mouth of the Piscataqua. On a fair day, the waterborne traffic under sail here makes an enjoyable sight. The river also carries its share of heavy commercial shipping.

To return to Fort McClary and your car, retrace your steps, walking west on Chaunceys Creek and Pepperrell roads after you have crossed the bridge and regained the mainland. The total round trip adds up to a good five-mile hike.

2. Mount Agamenticus/ York

From anywhere on the southern Maine coast between Kittery and Kennebunkport, the most imposing shape on the horizon is Mount Agamenticus, a seven-hundred-foot hill in the wooded uplands west of York. Agamenticus can be spotted from almost any point on the shoreline and is immediately apparent to northbound travelers as they crest the I-95 high-level bridge between Portsmouth and Kittery. A ledgy mound that resisted the glacial leveling that ground down so much of the Maine coast millennia ago, Agamenticus provides several good woods walks with commanding views of the coast. And on summer days when the beaches are crowded with

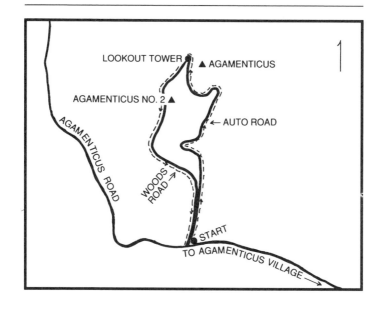

sun worshippers, the woods on Agamenticus are a cool, quiet respite from an over-busy world.

To reach the mountain, drive north or south on U.S. Route 1 to the Cape Neddick section of York, situated on a bend in the road. On the west side of the highway, watch for Mountain Road (sometimes called Agamenticus Road). Turn west here. Follow winding Mountain Road for about 1⅓ miles to an intersection with Chase's Pond Road. Keep right here and continue westward, staying left at a pronounced Y that you come upon shortly. Roughly 2¾ miles from the junction with Chase's Pond Road, the paved road ends where the summit auto road runs right. To your right is a small gravel parking area at the junction— park here.

To reach the summit, head up the paved road northward. Tall red and white pines, balsam, birch, and scattered oak border the road. These woods are full of game and birdlife. Moose, fox, deer, skunk, rabbit, and other species are commonly seen. Ring-necked pheasant, spruce grouse, the pileated woodpecker, and other large birds frequent the area, too. Less than a quarter mile from the parking area, you'll come to a shaded woods road to the left under an arch of balsams. Enter the woods here.

This attractive little road runs northwest and west along the right side of a depression, gradually pulling around to the left. Watch for deer or other animal tracks in the damp soil or snow, depending upon the time of year. Once you've made the bend, keep your eyes open for a path on the immediate right. Blazes indicate its beginning. Go right on the trail, which now runs briskly uphill to the north. The woodland growth thins out here, leaving mainly balsam and scrub oak. The path rises over a series of ledgy outcrops, pulls slightly to the right, and then, running northeastward, emerges on the summit parking area.

Make for the fire tower ahead to the north. The tower is manned irregularly in the summer, depending upon weather conditions. Go up the tower steps for some excellent views of the entire south-coastal region. If the towerman is present, it may be possible to visit the cabin. Knock and inquire.

To the northwest, you will see the rangy mass of Mount Hope in Sanford. On exceptionally clear days, especially in winter, you can see Mount Washington and the southern Presidential Range, more than one hundred miles away. In winter, the snowy, white caps of the Presidential Range are unmistakable. To the west is the relatively flat plain of eastern New Hampshire.

Coastal views are spectacular from here. The point of land far to the northeast is Fletcher's Neck at Biddeford Pool (beyond the large water tower). Kennebunk Beach, Moody Beach, and Ogunquit Beach run to the east and southeast. Well to the southeast is the distinctive profile of York's Nubble Light. If the weather is clear, Boon Island Light shows on the ledges, well out to sea. To the south, the famous Isles of Shoals are visible on many days.

The summit, site of a long-abandoned ski area, is worth exploring. When you're ready to descend, follow the auto road down. The road winds east, west, and then south to the parking area where you left your car. The round trip is about one mile and can be done in an hour, with ample time for visiting the fire tower. If you plan to climb the tower in winter, wear a warm windshell; as the highest point of an otherwise unobstructed coastal plain, Agamenticus really catches the wind in the colder months.

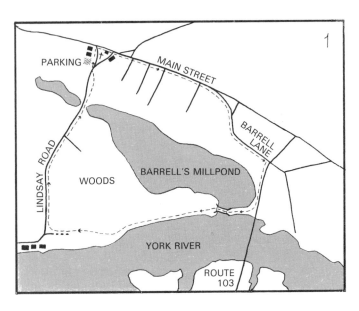

3. York Village

eil Rolde's book, *York Is Living History,* says it all: historic York will capture the interest of anyone who cares even a little about early American life. Only, in York, history isn't some musty abstraction. It's all around you: old homes, stores, warehouses, churches, and churchyards in a beautiful setting above a river, the harbor, and the sea.

There are many walks in York, but one of the most varied takes in both the town and the riverfront. Begin in York Village center at the junction of Main Street and Lindsay Road by Jefferds' Tavern. A few yards south on Lindsay Road you'll find off-street parking next to the Old Schoolhouse, built in 1745. On the opposite side of the road lies the Old Burying Ground, with some of the most fascinating weathered headstones in New England.

Back on Main Street, a whole cluster of historic structures lies along your route, and you may want to allow some extra time here. The First Parish Parsonage and the First Parish Church, the latter originally built in 1747, are attractive buildings. The old Courthouse, which now serves as Town Hall, was constructed in 1844.

Diagonally opposite and eastward, you'll see the George Ingraham House, dating from 1740. Close to it, on the hill, rests the well-known Old Gaol of York. This forbidding stone and timber relic, built in 1719, survives as a hoary reminder of Colonial criminal justice practices. The original jail was begun in 1653. It went through several modifications but proved too bitterly cold to house prisoners and was succeeded by the present structure.

Continue east and southeast on Main Street, shortly turning south on Barrell Lane, named after a York delegate to the Massachusetts Constitutional Convention. Bear right again on Route 103 heading toward the river.

To the left and east, the York River flows around Stage Neck to York Harbor. On your right, a breakwater separates Barrell's Millpond from the river. Turn right here and walk along the breakwater and cross the suspension bridge. The path now follows an attractive stretch of the river westward.

This trail passes briefly along the grassy riverbank and then pulls left and into the woods. After walking through mixed growth dominated by tall white pines, you soon meet a road at a big overhead sign. Bear right here and walk west to Lindsay Road. Go left at this main, paved road and walk the short distance to the river, where you'll see the Samuel Lindsay House, John Hancock Wharf, and the George Marshall Store. Each of these is an interesting relic of the Colonial period. Nearby are attractive views of wharves and the bridges over the York River.

Turn around here and retrace your steps along Lindsay Road toward town, passing several attractive older structures as you walk northwest toward the village center. The Samuel Moody Parsonage, dating from 1699, lies on your right shortly after you pass the northwest end of the millpond.

In minutes you return to your starting point. Jefferds' Tavern and the Old Schoolhouse are usually open to visitors at certain times during the summer months. The walker may also visit the Old Burying Ground. The ancient headstones here provide a unique chronicle of life and death in Colonial Maine. This area and the houses surrounding it are all worth some exploration before returning to your car. The entire walk around York is about two miles and can be done in not much over an hour.

4. Marginal Way/
Ogunquit

The short, splendid walk along Ogunquit's Marginal Way belongs on your itinerary whenever you're visiting Maine's southern coast.

Located right on U.S. Route 1 about twelve miles north of the Maine–New Hampshire border, Ogunquit boasts one of the finest beaches in Maine. The village also contains a delightful array of interesting shops, summer theatres, restaurants, galleries, and bookstores. And for those dedicated to walking, few pathways offer such majestic views seaward as does the Marginal Way.

A lonely, quiet place in winter, Ogunquit gets about as busy as it can stand in summer. It's a good

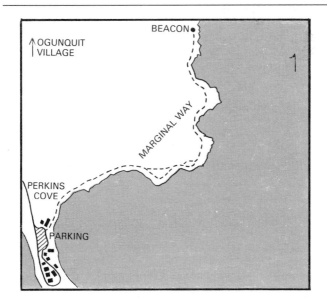

idea to park in the center of the village, make a foot tour of that area, and then walk south along Shore Road toward Perkins Cove. You'll pass more shops along the way.

The road to Perkins Cove veers left about one mile south of the village center and runs southeasterly down to the cove itself. A small fleet of work boats anchors here, as do several charters available for sport fishing. Dozens of little fishing shacks, some converted into shops or homes, dot the tiny spit of land that separates Perkins Cove from Oarweed Cove and the open Atlantic.

To walk the Marginal Way, head north along the edge of Oarweed Cove to the path that begins by Oarweed's Eating Place. The Marginal Way climbs gradually away from the shingle and turns toward the northeast. Moving through low scrub, you're soon well above the cliffs. The outlooks south over the water are fine. A number of turnouts lead right for better views.

If you're like most people, you'll probably want to walk along the headland in fair weather, but if you want to understand the real drama of the Maine coast, don't hesitate to make this walk when the tide is full and a storm sends the surf at full tilt toward the cliffs. You'll find it hard to settle for the placid warmth of a sandy beach once you've tramped the Marginal Way in heavy weather.

You soon turn more to the north as the path makes the circuit of the headland. Watch for some interesting folded metamorphic rock above the water-line here. More in the open now, you continue north, shortly reaching the beacon that marks the end of the way. Ahead to the north lies the clean, long strand of Ogunquit Beach.

Retracing your steps at a leisurely pace, perhaps with some time out to clamber about the rocks, will bring you back to your car. Walking the Marginal Way isn't strenuous—just beautiful. Whatever your age or condition, you'll enjoy it.

Note: If you walked down to Perkins Cove along Shore Road and you wish to return to Ogunquit

Village center, you may continue on an extension of the Marginal Way that stays above the shore beyond the beacon just mentioned. This section of the walk will bring you shortly out to Shore Road, where you turn right for the village center, or left to walk back down Shore Road to Perkins Cove. (This part of the route is otherwise not recommended, as development in recent years has absorbed most of the fine pasture and lawns through which it once passed.)

Walkers who descend to the rocks below the Marginal Way are reminded that conditions on the ledges are very slippery and that a strong undertow exists. People have been swept from these rocks during storms in recent years. Use caution if you descend below the established path.

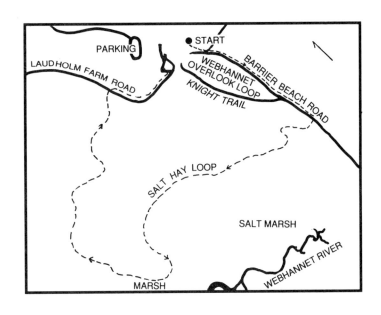

PARKING

START

LAUDHOLM FARM ROAD

BARRIER BEACH ROAD

WEBHANNET OVERLOOK LOOP

KNIGHT TRAIL

SALT HAY LOOP

SALT MARSH

WEBHANNET RIVER

MARSH

5. Wells National Estuarine Research Reserve at Laudholm Farm/Wells

Perched dramatically on a high meadow overlooking a salt marsh and the Atlantic Ocean, Laudholm Farm is a superbly restored nineteenth-century saltwater farm now open to walkers in all seasons. The 250-acre farm abuts the Rachel Carson National Wildlife Refuge and Laudholm State Park. The farm, the park, and the Carson Refuge together protect over fifteen hundred acres of vital shoreline, and are today known as the Wells National Estuarine Research Reserve, the first such reserve in northern New England. It was planned, organized, and brought into the federal system entirely through the initiative and efforts of local citizens.

To walk the trails of Laudholm Farm, leave I-95 at exit 2 and drive east to Wells Corner. At the lights, bear left and north on U.S. Route 1 and proceed about 1¾ miles to the second blinking light. Turn here onto Laudholm Farm Road. You soon come to a fork in the road, where you bear left and then right at the entrance to the reserve. The entrance road leads across the pastures to a parking area near the great barn.

Several excellent walkways wind through Laudholm Farm, and one could easily spend several days here and at the adjacent Carson preserve enjoying the various trails. The walk described below is known as the Salt Hay Loop and covers a one-and-a-half to two-hour walk over a two-mile circuit. Part of the route crosses wet ground, so be sure to wear waterproof foot gear. The walk begins by the flagpole in the farmyard. Cross the road and walk southeast along the cut swath through the high pasture. The trail follows a row of posts. The hiker has excellent views in this section out over Webhannet Marsh, Laudholm and Drakes Island beaches, and the Atlantic. A bench marks Webhannet Outlook at the far end of the pasture.

From the outlook, the trail meanders downward and to the east through brushy pasture, with the remains of a disused orchard to the right. Shortly, you arrive at a junction where the Knight Trail (which you're following) meets Barrier Beach Road. Turn right and southeast on this old woods road. You'll continue to descend toward the marsh and ocean. Birch, maple, and aspen arch over the pathway.

As the trail levels out, watch for a wooden walkway on your left and another trail departing to the right. You will come back to this spot momentarily, but for now, proceed farther southeast through an area between the estuaries of the Little River (left) and the Webhannet River (right). You are likely to see species of both land and aquatic birds from here.

Going through a gate at the end of Barrier Beach Road, you cross a roadway and follow the path to Laudholm Beach (left). Please avoid trespassing on the private property adjoining the path. If you're an inveterate beach stroller, exploring this stretch of beach can be fascinating, regardless of the season. The walk continues by backtracking from the beach, through the gate, and up the path you descended until you reach the wooden walkway on your right. Turn *left* and southwest here through a boggy, abandoned orchard. The path makes several turns through apple trees and among young aspens and clusters of gray birch. Prickly barberry bushes line both sides of the path.

The trail soon emerges into a brushy field bordered on the south by more of the apple trees. Deer paths cross the field at various angles, and one should be careful not to mistake them for the regular trail, which is marked by blazes of colored tape. The path dips into a low area of dense beech and apple, then re-enters the pasture, continuing west. The trail next runs southwest, with occasional views of the farmhouse to the northwest and of Webhannet Marsh. The trail then widens gradually and continues south and southeast through an open range of swamp maples. Great black fish crows live here and move with loud commotion from tree to tree.

You pass a giant shagbark hickory momentarily. The trail then meanders generally southeast and east through wet, low ground, where your waterproof shoes or boots will prove their usefulness. The walk-way comes to a series of planks and then a board-walk leading to Salt Hay Overlook, an observation platform on the west side of the marsh, which is drained by the Webhannet River. The platform, surrounded by young maples, scattered birch, and cordgrass, stands well out into the life of the marsh. Meadowsweet, salt hay, and cattails grow here in profusion.

This marsh provides and excellent example of the utility of intertidal estuaries. The marsh is fed by runoff from the higher ground to the west and north-west. Marine organisms enter the marsh through the incoming tidal flux, though that is limited in this par-ticular marsh by a tidegate at Drakes Island Road, which inhibits the inflow of salt water. Rich organic and mineral sediments accumulate and are washed about and mixed within the marsh, providing a source of nutrition for many plant and animal types. *Where Rivers Meet the Sea,* a publication of National Ocean Service/National Oceanic and Atmospheric Administration, reports: "Estuaries are among the most biologically productive systems on earth. More than two-thirds of the fish and shellfish commercially harvested in coastal waters spend part or all of their lives in estuaries. Millions of people enjoy fishing, boating, and related activities and also benefit from the food and employment created by the resources nurtured in estuarine systems. Estuaries also provide other benefits, including storm and flood protection and pollution control, at no cost to taxpayers."

Probably you have also noticed that this estuarine

area provides a home to many animal and bird species, all of which find readily available sources of food and shelter here. It is precisely because estuarine zones play such a vital ecological role in the natural environment that more of us must raise our voices to prevent the destruction of such lands in the name of "development" or "progress."

From the outlook, retrace your steps to dry ground, watching for the trail to bear left at a junction. From the junction, the trail runs southwest and west, gradually pulling around to the north under a giant white pine with thirteen or fourteen separate trunks. The path widens to a woods road here, arriving soon in an open grove of red oak. Deer abound in this terrain, and you are very likely to come upon several grazing if you walk quietly. I have seen deer every time I've walked in this preserve, sometimes as many as half a dozen. Keep your eyes open.

Crossing a seasonal brook, you begin to walk due north through low woods. Hemlock, some big maples, and wood ferns border the trail. A dense beech and alder swamp lies to the right. You next pull eastward into a field and walk northeast along the edge of the woods, shortly tending around to the northwest again and re-entering the periphery of the woods. The last section of the trail follows an old built-up roadbed and emerges on a paved road in front of Laudholm farmhouse. Walk up the hill to the right to reach your starting point.

Waterproof foot gear should be worn on this hike regardless of season. If you make the walk in June, July, or August, insect repellent is a must. For more information on the National Estuarine Reserve System, write or call: Laudholm Trust, P.O. Box 1007, Wells, ME 04090, (207) 646-4521. Guided walks are conducted at Laudholm on varying schedules; call for information. The reserve is currently open in daylight hours from Tuesday through Saturday, closed Sunday and Monday.

6. Rachel Carson National Wildlife Refuge/Wells

The word *ecology* belonged strictly in the lexicon of the specialist until, in 1962, a quiet, unprepossessing woman wrote a book entitled *Silent Spring*. Nearly two decades later, Rachel Carson's words have reached millions of people and sparked worldwide environmental awareness. In *The Sea Around Us, Edge of the Sea,* and *Silent Spring,* Carson wrote, in terms that everyone could understand, of the profound interconnection between all living things on this beautiful,

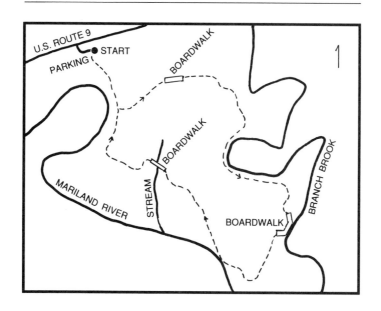

troubled planet. Her writing brought to our awareness the fragile, beleaguered nature of our shores and wetlands, and she made us see how, when we filled in, drained, or poisoned a marsh, we were destroying the natural foundations of our own lives. If generations to come have the awareness and good sense to protect and extend the wild areas along our shores, and to use these riparian zones more wisely than earlier generations have, much credit must go to Rachel Carson. In a popular sense, it was her solitary, insistently rational voice that awoke so many of us from our slumber and made us see that we have been destroying the planet we call home. Nothing could be more fitting than that a fine section of prime coastal wetland should be named in her honor.

The Rachel Carson National Wildlife Refuge is a collection of coastal lands strung along the southern

Maine coast. The portion included here, located in Wells, provides an unspoiled, protected habitat for many animal and avian species common to southern Maine. The refuge protects a fine natural salt marsh that is, itself, a vital stopping-off place for migratory birds of all kinds. On a spring or summer morning, the woods of the Carson Refuge fairly ring with birdsong. Although it is just moments from the road, one walks into an unspoiled world that is tranquil, yet vital and interesting. The route described below is a self-guiding, interpretive nature trail that winds its way through very at-

tractive woods and then along the borders of a great marsh.

To walk the trails of this portion of the Carson National Wildlife Refuge, take U.S. Route 1 to Wells. From Wells Corner, drive north on Route 1, bearing right and northeast on Maine Route 9 about 1½ miles north of Wells center. The refuge lies about one-half mile from the junction of Route 1 and Maine Route 9 and is marked by a large brown sign on the right side of the road. Turn right into a short drive that brings you to a parking area by the warden's residence. An information board with trail maps and other notices stands to the right of the parking lot next to the trailhead. Recently, the main loop trail around the reserve has been graded and filled, and it can now be negotiated by persons in wheelchairs. With this upgrading, the following route is probably the most accessible genuine woods experience for physically challenged people on the Maine coast. The walk takes about an hour.

From the parking lot head across the gravel road southeast into the woods. To the right, the long, meandering course of the Merriland River lies down a steep bank. The first of eleven marked outlooks comes up shortly, with good views over the river to the northwest. The riverbank is dotted with fallen trees that have toppled into the water, their root systems exposed by the steady erosion of the river. If you have picked up a trail map at the information board, you will find an interesting description of the terrain and wildlife keyed to each of the eleven outlooks.

Turn left and east now through a grove of large, old white pines and scattered red pines. Dark and shady, these groves play host to a wide variety of native and migrating birds. Hemlocks shortly become predominant, and you cross a small footbridge under the branches of one of these giant evergreens. To the right are low, wet acres full of spinulose wood ferns. Proceeding through mixed growth, you pull around to the southeast and south, arriving soon at a raised platform with excellent views into the salt marsh. The erratic meanderings of Branch Brook lie before you. From here, you can also get a sense of how large this intertidal area is. You may also begin to see some of the active avian wildlife busy in the marsh. I have watched kingfishers hard at work over the brook here on many occasions.

The path next makes an arc around the brook, gradually turning eastward. A dozen large trees have fallen into the stream here, the bank having been literally washed out from under them by erosive action. Eventually, the stream will cut its way through the banking at the top end of this meander and will flow more or less straight again, leaving a stagnant oxbow pond where the old channel once looped. In the woods to your right grow fir, pine, beech, and maple. Indian pipes may be found here, seasonally, in the underbrush. A giant northern red oak leans over the trail.

Turning toward the south, you pass another platform and descend shortly to a boardwalk that drops into the marsh to reach an observation platform perched at the edge of Branch Brook. One can observe here the strength of the tidal current— whether ebbing or flowing. Salt pannes, shallow pools of saline water in the marsh grass, trap marine life that then supports other species. Snowy egrets may be seen fishing these little shallow pools in summer. Salt hay (*Spartina patens*) and smooth cordgrass (*Spartina alterniflora*, Loiseleur) grow luxuriantly on both banks of the brook. A bench on the platform provides a place to rest and observe birdlife.

A short march southwestward leads to another outlook over the junction of the two streams you have seen earlier. Far out over the marsh to the southeast, you can see the rolling surf of the open Atlantic in clear weather. You also have excellent views northwestward up the Merriland River. The marsh is broad here, with dense forest on its west side. This section of the marsh can be observed as you walk northwestward. Deer come down to the banks on the far side of the stream, particularly in winter, and sometimes can be watched for hours as they feed at the edge of the marsh. Under a great white pine, a memorial to Rachel Carson has been erected. Ducks swim in the pools.

White oak and maple are interspersed with pine and more hemlock in this section of the forest. Great blue heron and other wading shorebirds may be seen here. The trail curves and dips to a footbridge, crossing a seasonal brook. The runoff from the high tableland along which you have been walking is fed to the marsh, where it is distributed to the streams and on to the sea. One of the most important features of a tidal salt marsh is this constant filtering and interchange of the products of both land and water—upland drainage and dilute seawater. The last views back down the marsh to the ocean are along this stretch.

Walking first northwest and then due north, you complete the final link of the trail, which now closely follows the upper reaches of the Merriland. In just a moment you come to the outlook where you began the walk and continue north to the parking area.

To preserve the natural beauty of the refuge, please leave nothing behind. If you've found this to be as impressive and refreshing a walk as I do, keep in mind Rachel Carson's words, which appear on the trail map and which are taken from *The Sea Around Us:* "All the life of the planet is interrelated . . . and each species has its own ties to others, and . . . all are related to the earth."

7. SCARBOROUGH MARSH/
SCARBOROUGH

However well you know Maine, you have to stop and think a moment when told that a three-thousand-acre wildlife management area exists in the most settled part of its coast. This great plot of terrain, reserved to the rhythms of nature, happens to rest just a few miles from Maine's largest city.

The sizable piece of unsettled ground we're describing is Scarborough Marsh. Owned by the Maine Department of Inland Fisheries and Wildlife, the marsh includes the site of a Maine Audubon Society nature center. In addition to its educational functions, the nature center furnishes a starting point for a short but highly interesting tramp into the marsh.

On any given day, the tiny Audubon Nature Center may be the scene of a variety of programs—canoe trips through the marsh, classes on marsh ecology, special wildlife displays, or lectures. And there is much to teach.

A marsh seems to be, to most minds, a useless bit of watery ground. After all, nothing productive happens there, right? Audubon's nature center shows visitors that things are quite the reverse. Marshes are home to an incredible number of species, above and below the waterline.

Coastal marshes play a major role in the development of fish and shellfish cultures. Some sixty species of fish and shellfish live in the Scarborough Marsh. According to Audubon's guide to the marsh, a mere eight acres of the marshland produced forty-three thousand pounds of clam meat in a single year.

A marsh serves as the site of a complex interaction between land and sea, trapping sediment, pro-

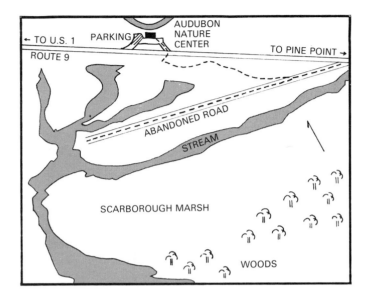

viding food and breeding grounds for birds, animals, and marine life, and serving as a natural safeguard against flooding. Not bad for a piece of "useless" ground. And all this miraculously interwoven activity can be witnessed by any coastal hiker willing to walk slowly and observe carefully.

You can walk the marsh from a number of places. The route described here begins opposite the nature center on Maine Route 9, about a mile east of U.S. Route 1 in Scarborough. The marsh, if you want to check your map, is roughly bounded by Route 9 on the south; by Route 1 on the west and north; and by Route 207, Prouts Neck, and the Atlantic on the east. Park in the lot at the Audubon Nature Center.

As you enter the marsh, the trail turns immediately toward the southeast and passes clumps of cattails. Only a few grow here, as cattails are native to freshwater marsh. Not far beyond on your left, an abandoned den, possibly the former home of a muskrat, hides under the scrub.

You continue southeast and east along a path now bordered by salt hay and, closer to the water, cordgrass. Red-winged blackbirds circle and chatter overhead, expressing their territorial claims and warning you away from nearby nests.

If you've slowed down enough to leave civilization back with your car, you'll be struck here by the very different world that characterizes the marsh. Only several yards away from the roar of traffic on Route 9, another order of activity goes busily forward. Insects make their rounds, birds fly about on the serious business of food getting and nest building, plants compete for space and light, and animals such as the muskrat scurry about largely unseen.

Turning more southeasterly again and crossing a small mound, you reach the remnants of an old road that once cut through the marsh. Bear left at this spot, walking toward the bridge and the main road. Two streams here carry nutrient-rich water from inland to the marine life attached to rocks and in the stream beds.

Next, head back along the old road toward the center of the marsh. To the south, woods come down to the marsh, and you may see large white birds take wing there. These beautiful snowy egrets, along with

herons and glossy ibises, are usually a part of the summer bird population at Scarborough. (Southern birds, the egret and ibis have summered in Maine only recently.)

Moving farther to the southwest along the road, which has nearly been overgrown, watch for other shorebirds. Willets, yellowlegs, and semipalmated sandpipers are common. Walking here, I have seen an occasional black duck in summer, too.

The path ends shortly at a shallow washout. Return to the nature center via the same route. Your round trip will be less than one mile, but will require one-and-a-half to two hours if you go slowly enough to take in all the marsh life around you. Wear waterproof walking shoes or boots if possible (particularly in spring). A pocket guide, available at the nature center, will add to your enjoyment of the marsh— and bring along your field glasses.

If you enjoy canoeing, you might consider renting a canoe at the Audubon building. A half-day trip up and down the tidal stream north of Maine Route 9 can be a fascinating way to explore this great marsh further. Enquire at the nature center for information.

8. PEAKS ISLAND/
PORTLAND

Casco Bay, that arm of the Atlantic on which Portland, Maine's largest city, fronts, is nearly two hundred square miles in area. Within this enormous bay rest a reported 365 islands, named, not suprisingly, the Calendar Islands. Some would point out that these are not all really islands, and that a fair number' are actually tidal ledges that are submerged a part of each day. Probably about two hundred are actually islands in the strictest sense of the word, and, of those, about 130 are of habitable size. Still, 130 interesting islands in a single beautiful bay is an impressive statistic by any standard, and on many of these islands there are rewards for the dedicated walker.

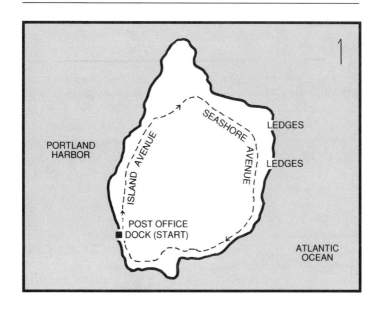

Peaks is one of the most populous of the big Casco Bay islands. It's also just a short boat ride from the mainland, and easily reached year-round. Although it's just a commute to those who live there, the boat ride to Peaks is a pleasant, interesting trip for most of us and provides a scenic introduction to the slower paced offshore life some are lucky enough to live.

Catch the Peaks boat at the Ferry Terminal, junction of Franklin and Commercial streets on the Portland Waterfront. Casco Bay Island Transit District operates island service about every hour during the summer, somewhat less frequently in the winter months. For information, call (207) 774-7871. A printed schedule of sailings is available at the CBITD office in the new Casco Bay Ferry Terminal Building. A parking garage is located adjacent to the pier.

The trip to Peaks takes about twenty minutes and runs up the middle of Portland Harbor. On the way out, you'll see the commercial docks, fish piers, and shipbuilding activities of both Portland and South Portland. Fort Gorges is the squat, military-looking structure on Diamond Ledge to the left in mid-harbor. It was built under the direction of then Secretary of War Jefferson Davis just before he quit the post to become the leader of the Confederacy. Fort Gorges was never garrisoned; changes in sea-going military tactics rendered it obsolete before it was completed. Over to the south and southeast are the big oil terminals of South Portland. A major oil pipeline runs from Portland to Montreal, and from these unloading points the oil is pumped northward to warm the Canadian winters.

Once you are well away from the mainland, you can spy Portland Head Light on its lofty headland to the east-southeast, above the channel that separates it from Cushing Island. Little and Great Diamond islands are to your left as you approach Peaks, and you can look up the channel northward toward Long Island and the Chebeagues. The small island to your right with a couple of houses perched on it is House Island, more or less abandoned for a while but now

actively inhabited again. The boat will drop you off at
Jones Wharf on the southwest side of Peaks in the
center of the island's little settlement.

From the wharf, walk uphill to the corner and turn
left by the shops on Island Avenue, which is the main
artery of the settled part of the island. The only grocery
store on the island is here, and if you didn't bring food
and drink with you, this will be your last chance to put
something in your daypack. Continue northward along
Island Avenue, with occasional views of Portland across
the bay. In one-quarter mile the road bends to the
right and runs uphill. Go up the hill, shortly passing a
schoolhouse and playground, and keep left on Pleasant
Avenue. Follow this street past houses and scattered
cottages for about one-half mile, until you come to an
attractive old three-gabled house on your right. This is
the Trefethen Homestead, built in 1844, and this section of the island is known simply as Trefethen. Turn
right here on Trefethen Avenue and go uphill around a
corner. This road soon intersects another street to
the right. Take this right turn by an A-shaped telephone
pole and head southeast and east on Ocean Avenue.

If you've walked this far, you have probably noticed
that Peaks is not an ordinary place. The architecture of
the island is varied and fun to examine. Yards often

possess an interesting collection of old cars, brought
here in their younger days and now used for parts.
Old dogs amble up and meet you on the road, and
people say hello and wave in a way that mainlanders
do not. Although still very much connected with the
city over the waters, Peaks is like many Maine islands
in its quiet and lack of pretense. Indeed, one of the
things I always notice first on an island is the absence of mainland noises, and it's a welcome relief.

The next section of the walk is along the less
developed ocean side of Peaks. Pleasant stands of
spruce, aspen, and fragrant white pine line the road.
Your first views of the open ocean lie ahead. The road
descends eastward here, and you pass a small pond
surrounded by staghorn sumac on the right just
before turning more to the south. Gray birch and
dense bittersweet border the street. In moments you
walk opposite Spar Cove, a pretty lagoon bordered by
boulders and low ledges.

The road arches around the cove and continues
in a southerly direction, and here you can spot some
of the many islands in the bay across the water to the
east and northeast. Long Island is to the north, with
Great Chebeague beyond it. Cliff and Jewell islands
are to the northeast. Inner Green Island, Green
Island Reef, and Outer Green Island are to the east.
Junk of Pork is just south of Outer Green. As the
road runs above the shore, heading steadily south,
you will see Ram Island and Ram Island Ledges (with
lighthouse) ahead. Cushing Island is the larger landmass to the southwest.

You come to a street on your right soon, and
opposite it is a good place to sit on the ledges over the
ocean. At low tide, shoreline exploration is possible
here, but exercise caution if you walk below the
riprap. The kelp-covered ledges can be very slippery.
Examination of the rock formations will reveal folded,
metamorphosed shales and sandstones, iron oxide,
and basaltic dikes, all laid down millions of years ago.

As you walk southward, the road runs by a long,
low swampy area grown up with cattails and dominated by a fortification buried in a hillside to the

west. Aspens and thick brush surround the marsh. Land birds and shorebirds nest or forage here. It's quiet: only the sound of birdsong, or the wind and ocean. If you walk this stretch of road in winter, open to the Atlantic as it is, you're likely to get a good buffeting or soaking. The wind off the open ocean can be quite fierce here in a winter storm, but a walk on a dry, sunny, and very brisk winter's day can be a tonic and a great weekend escape.

The road now pulls to the southwest. The great northern cliffs of Cushing Island are now on your left. Whitehead Passage is the channel between Peaks and Cushing. The road now turns alternately west and south as it saws its way among the big old cottages of another era. Stay on Seashore Avenue to Whitehead Avenue to Island Avenue as you come around this southern tip of the island. Once on Island Avenue, you walk through the residential section of the village to the west and then north to Jones Wharf.

Because there is not much shelter on Peaks, winter walkers should wear warm clothing and carry foul-weather gear. A small waiting room has been erected on the pier for those taking the boats. A restaurant next to the pier tends to be open on a restricted schedule during the winter months.

9. Mackworth Island/ Falmouth

Mackworth Island is a small landmass on the west side of Casco Bay just off a peninsula in the extreme southeast corner of the town of Falmouth. The island, which is home to the Baxter School for the Deaf, is connected to the mainland by a long causeway. Though not a large island, Mackworth is highly visible from the mainland, especially from Portland's Eastern Promenade, where it can be seen directly to the north. The center of the island is occupied by the buildings and athletic fields of the Baxter School, but the periphery is circled by an excellent trail that follows the shoreline all the way and offers a very attractive woods walk, plus striking views of Casco Bay. Because of its close proximity to Portland, the walk around Mackworth is easily accessible throughout the year.

To reach the island, drive north from Portland on I-295, turning right and north on U.S. Route 1 at Martin Point. Route 1 crosses the Presumpscot River just beyond Martin Point. Once past the river, watch for Andrews Avenue on your right. Turn down Andrews Avenue, which becomes the causeway to the island. At the end of the causeway, just as you arrive on the island, a small parking area is to the left by the guard shack. Park fully off the road here.

The trail departs northward from this small parking lot through a grove of red and white pine, beech, and white birch. The path stays close to the water, and great oaks lean over the trail at waterside. You shortly walk through a pretty grove of dense white pine. Some of the trees are tangled with bittersweet vines. In a quarter mile you reach the first headland, with good views up the coast by a clump of birches. The coastal shores of Falmouth, Cumberland, and Yarmouth are visible from here.

The trail pulls next toward the east in another birch grove, and you come to an open field. Don't enter the field, but follow the path around a sharp turn to the left and into the woods once again. After moving through a shady corridor, you again skirt the shore, with views to the west. Passing more stands of red pine and oak, you arrive at the second prominent headland by a large oak. Here the outlook is to the north. The tiny islands directly northward are known

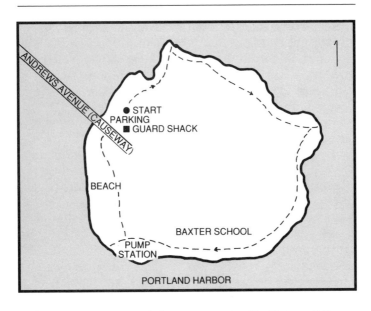

as The Brothers, and there are actually three of them, though usually only two are visible. Farther north-ward, in line with The Brothers, is long, narrow Clapboard Island. Way up the channel to the north-east are Little and Great Chebeague islands. If you enjoy shoreline exploration, at low tide you can descend to the intertidal zone beneath the path and walk for some distance.

The main trail continues east along the shore above a small beach for one-quarter mile, and then swings gradually toward the southeast, passing a trail that comes in on the right. Pine and spruce provide cover in this section. Shortly, views of Casco Bay open up to the east. The little island to the immediate northeast across the channel is Cow Island. Behind it is Long Island. Great Diamond and Little Diamond islands lie east and southeast. Fort Gorges, a Civil War fortification that was never used, stands alone to the southeast. A stone jetty runs offshore to the left.

The trail soon begins to make the turn around the southeast corner of the island below the buildings of Baxter School. Views open up to Portland's Eastern Prom and over to the docks of South Portland far away to the south. It can be interesting to stop at one of the open spots along the shore and watch the sizable boat and ship traffic moving through the bay. Continue walking westward, with the shore to your immediate left and the school grounds on the right. At the southwest corner of the island, when you have passed the school buildings, you begin to move away from the shore and stay more above the water, arriving shortly at a small brick pumping station in the shape of a little tower. Here you can either continue on the main path or bear left and descend to a beach. Golden hardhack and fleabane flourish in this zone. Walk northwest along this shore, enjoying the views over to the Eastern Prom and to Martin Point. The trail continues up a banking near the causeway and brings you out to the road by the parking lot.

The distance around the loop is about 1¼ miles and can be done in an hour of moderately paced walking. In all but the height of summer, it is usually a good idea to carry a windshell when making this walk as protection from the strong breezes off Casco Bay.

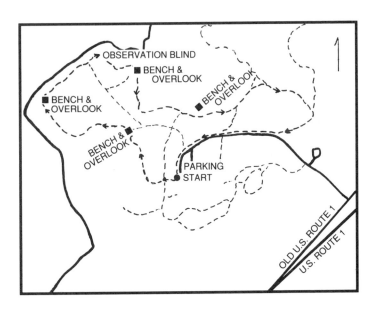

OBSERVATION BLIND

BENCH &
OVERLOOK

BENCH &
OVERLOOK

BENCH &
OVERLOOK

BENCH &
OVERLOOK

PARKING
START

OLD U.S. ROUTE 1

U.S. ROUTE 1

10. GILSLAND FARM SANCTUARY/FALMOUTH

Just minutes from the center of Maine's largest city, Gilsland Farm is located on the west side of a peninsula in Falmouth. Despite its proximity to the city, Gilsland Farm provides splendid walking through rolling fields and woodlands in an atmosphere as tranquil and beautiful as you are likely to find anywhere. The farm site is also headquarters of the Maine Audubon Society, which is housed in a unique, solar-heated building in the southeast corner of the sanctuary. The building contains meeting facilities, a library, and a shop that offers an interesting selection of nature books, maps, guides, and binoculars. A map of all trails in the sanctuary is available here, as is the useful booklet, *Natural Communities of Gilsland Farm.*

Gilsland Farm is just off U.S. Route 1 on a small loop road (watch for sign) on the west side of Route 1 opposite the junction of Route 1 and Maine Route 88. The preserve is about 2½ miles north of Portland via Martins Point.

The route described here, which follows the periphery of the southern half of the preserve, begins at the southwest corner of the main parking lot at the visitors center. From the trailhead, walk west, descending quickly into a shallow depression thickly grown up with sugar maples, birch, and red oak. In just a few yards you cross another trail, continuing straight ahead and descending farther into a boggy area laced with ferns. The trail shortly pulls around to the north and northwest, crosses two footbridges, and emerges into an open pasture known as West Meadow.

Gilsland was operated as a farm after the turn of the century by David Moulton. An attorney and horticulturist, Moulton planted spruce, maple, apple, and other trees, along with lilacs, forsythia, and grapes. The meadows are kept open, and at West Meadow the pathway follows a mowed swath up the pasture rise in front of you. From the height of land, you can look southward along the shore of the Presumpscot River.

The trail runs first northwestward and then southwest around the edge of the field, bordered to

your left with sumac, ragweed, and horsetails. In a few minutes you'll turn northwestward as the trail now skirts the river's edge under a canopy of giant oaks. You arrive soon at an outlook in the westernmost quarter of the sanctuary, offering excellent views up and down the Presumpscot. A number of shorebirds frequent the sanctuary's perimeter, and you may see yellowlegs, snowy egrets, great blue herons, and a variety of ducks.

From the outlook, you'll walk northeast above the river past alternating clusters of aspen and sumac. One can see far to the northeast here, over the entire expanse of West Meadow. Watch for a trail junction where you drop left and northwest in a short loop down to the riverbank. Your destination here is a river blind in a grove of oaks. Here, shielded from sight, you can sit and watch the activity of ducks and other shorebirds in season. Continue around the loop, which rises quickly to another height of land with views out over the mudflats that are prominent on the preserve's west shore.

Dropping south and east, the trail skirts the

marsh, passes a row of crabapples, and enters the woods. Walking under a cluster of giant oaks, you continue east and then north in an arc sheltered by birch, maple, and occasional pine and fir. Watch for a lookout bench on your left, where there are excellent views out to the marsh and river. This is a good spot for photographers, particularly in autumn.

In this wooded section of the preserve, a variety of animal and bird life makes its home. Red and gray squirrels, white-tailed deer, raccoon, skunk, red fox, woodchuck, and vole live here. Many species of native and migratory land birds will be seen, and personnel at the visitors center can provide advice on which types are currently active.

The last section of this walk now runs out of the woods eastward and drops briefly to a depression, where you cross a footbridge. There are good views here through spindly maples out to the marsh and river—the prospect is particularly attractive in late afternoon. You now begin to climb slightly toward North Meadow, coming soon to a Y in the pathway. Keep right here, walking across the pasture in a southeasterly direction. Ahead, the community garden, barn, and education center lie near the road on which you entered the preserve. The route now loops to the west of these buildings and comes to the road. Turn right here and walk the short distance back to the parking area and visitors center.

If the Audubon Society building is open when you visit, I suggest you show your appreciation for the opportunity to walk this marvelous preserve by making a small contribution or becoming a member. Your support enables Maine Audubon to maintain not only the Gilsland Sanctuary, but also six other sanctuaries around the state. Contributions from each of us help ensure that these wildlands will remain secure and open for public use in years to come.

11. Bradbury Mountain State Park/ Pownal

Not *on* the sea, but close to it, Bradbury Mountain in Pownal provides an appealing upland base for walks in the coastal area. The mountain itself is at the center of one of the nicest small state parks in Maine. Excellent camping and picnic facilities are available for those who would spend a day or longer here walking over the mountain or hiking on some of the trails in nearby Freeport. Pownal lies more of less equidistant from Portland, Brunswick, and the lakes to the west and is a pleasant place to camp if you will be hiking anywhere within this southern-Maine triangle. This is, in any case, a place to come when you want a quiet, beautiful walk over easy grades with clear-weather views across the coastal plain to the sea. Bradbury Mountain State Park is rarely crowded, with the exception of a few weekends in high summer and in foliage season. If you visit during the week, even in summer, you're likely to have the terrain mostly to yourself. The park is equally attractive in winter, and it is possible to snowshoe and cross-country ski some of the trails as well as hike. A small fee is charged for entry in high summer, particularly on weekends.

To reach the mountain, drive west from Freeport on Maine Route 136, the first main road running west off Main Street north of L.L. Bean. After crossing above I-95, bear left sharply and follow the signs to Pownal Center. At the four corners in Pownal, bear right and north on Maine Route 9 and arrive at the park in less than a mile above the intersection. The warden's house is by the park entrance. Maps can be obtained and campground reservations made here.

The trail network at Bradbury Mountain has been

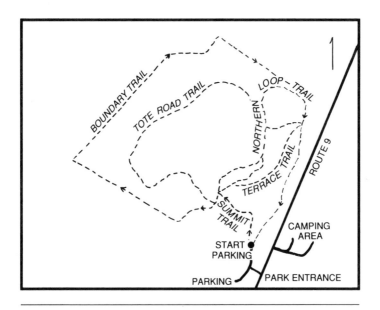

enlarged substantially since the first edition of this
book, and there are now several routes suitable to
varying levels of ability. The walk described in these
pages is the longest continuous path in the park and
follows the outer park boundaries nearly all the way.
The route is composed of the Summit Trail, the Boundary Trail, and the lower end of the Northern Loop.

Begin on the west side of the picnic area by the
main parking lot, behind the warden's house. There
are picnic tables, a water source, and toilets here for
public use. From the trail signs, you head northwest
and north as the path meanders up the grades of
Bradbury Mountain. The trail winds through tall,
majestic hemlocks, gradually working its way around
to the west and south. You will cross a series of steps
and bits of exposed ledge before emerging southward
on the bare summit ledges of the mountain, nearly five
hundred feet above sea level.

From the ledges there are broad, fine views eastward and to the south over the relatively flat plain
between here and the ocean on the other side of
Freeport. On clear days you can spot the coastline.
Farther to the south you'll see the edge of Casco Bay

and Portland. This is a very delightful place to have your lunch on a sunny day.

Behind the summit, the Boundary Trail departs west and southwest, descending through sparse white oaks. The trail runs southwest for a while, descending slightly until it comes to a rough stone wall. Here you turn west and right, following the wall and soon crossing through it. The route now descends farther, dropping down to the west in mixed-growth climax forest rich with the smell of balsam. The trail crosses a low spot on some logs and then begins to climb slightly, with a new stone wall coming in on the left. In minutes the trail reaches the corner boundary and turns right and northeast along the stone wall in thick balsam woods where bold little black-capped chickadees flit from branch to branch.

As you continue toward the northeast, you descend slowly and pass a cutover area on your left. Another section of stone wall is passed, and then the trail turns eastward, moving through a low, wet spot bisected by a seasonal brook. You now begin to march uphill again, reaching still another wall of weathered gray stone by a pasture. Here you pull sharply southeast, climbing farther before walking into open deciduous forest.

The trail now runs over a number of hummocks, coming soon to the Northern Loop Trail, on which you turn left and toward the southeast. This trail, which follows an old road, is broad and well lit. You pass through another wall as you move nearly on the level toward the south, where the Ski Trail and the Terrace Trail come in on your right. Some ledges, colorful with lichens, soon appear on the right. You can now proceed briskly due south, and, after passing an old stone structure on the left, you reach the park's athletic field and the parking area.

Winter hikers will find this loop of about $2\frac{1}{4}$ miles an attractive snowshoe walk. The Tote Road Trail and its continuation, the Ski Trail and lower Northern Loop, can be cross-country skied from the summit of Bradbury Mountain by experienced ski-tourers.

12. Mast Landing Sanctuary/Freeport

In use since the 1700s, Mast Landing and the area around it are closely bound up with the historical settlement of the Maine coast. While still a part of Massachusetts Bay Colony, Maine became a major provider of ship timber and masts to the rest of the world. Mast Landing and its environs were associated with both masting and shipbuilding. A grist mill, sawmill, and other operations were carried out here close to the Mill Dam, remnants of which still survive. The Millmaster's House, built by Abner Dennison in 1795, stands today on the east side of the current trail network, and relics of farming dating from early in this century are also found. This beautifully wooded and historic tract was given to the Maine Audubon Society by the L.M.C. Smith family in 1962. Mast Landing Sanctuary provides an ecologically oriented camp for children in the summer, and a site for enjoyable walking throughout the year.

To visit Mast Landing Sanctuary, take Dow Street east from the center of Freeport, directly opposite the L.L. Bean retail store. Shortly you bear left and northeast on Flying Point Road. Watch for a sign on the left in a hollow, and turn left on Upper Mast Landing Road. Cresting a hill immediately, you bear right on a gravel road into the sanctuary and park at a lot on your left as you enter.

This walk follows what is known as the Loop Trail, a circuit that wanders more than a mile and a half through the heart of the preserve. Nearly level all the way, the Loop Trail makes not only a fine woods walk but also an excellent route for cross-country skiers or snowshoers in winter. The trail begins by the signboard at the north end of the parking area and moves north and northwest over old meadows and orchard land dotted with apple trees. At the end of the field, the trail enters the woods by a grove of young aspens.

Continuing northeastward, you pass under two big sugar maples and go through a stone wall, passing The Cut-Off to your right. The trail follows an old farm road now and runs along a shaded ridge, passing a cellar hole among some aspens to the left. Red oak, beech, and red pine form a canopy over the path. Poplar and black cherry are also found in small stands. This little ridge is probably the highest point in the sanctuary and has a cathedral-like quality to it. The trail descends gradually into balsam, red spruce, and hemlock woods, and you come to a little turnout on the left where there is a bench. Resting here in the silence for a few moments, you will gradually attune your ear to the busy chatter of birdlife, which may include black-throated green warblers, black-capped chickadees, eastern kingbirds, hairy woodpeckers, and the occasional broad-winged hawk. Barred owls and great blue herons have been seen in the sanctuary, too.

From the bench turnout, step back to the main Loop Trail and walk east and southeast through a splendid grove of close-grown white pine. The trail soon runs above a densely vegetated boggy area through which the Mill Stream flows. The upland that you have been walking drains into the bog, which, in turn, feeds the Mill Stream as it supplies the headwater of the Harraseeket River. The narrow Mill Stream isn't very large or impressive as it moves through the sanctuary, but by the time the Harraseeket reaches the ocean, it has formed a major bay nearly a mile wide. While it meanders through the north and east quarters of the sanctuary, the Mill Stream provides a resource for mink, beaver, white-tailed deer, and fisher. The path of the Mill Stream is difficult to see from here when summer vegetation is lush, but you will get a closer look later, by the Mill Dam or via the Stream Spur.

Passing the Deer Run Trail, which comes in on your right, you continue to walk southeastward through a long alley of balsam and white pine. Shortly you will see an unmarked, grassy trail to your left. This is the Stream Spur, which takes you directly down to Mill Stream. If you are interested in stream-side ecology, it will be worth the time to make this brief side trip.

On the main trail, you pass beneath a telephone line and curve southwestward through more dense, coniferous forest. Passing the Bench Loop on your right, you continue walking easily southward as the trail broadens in mixed growth. Turning eastward in a moment, you emerge in open pasture. Bear right and walk southward again, and you soon pass by the sanctuary's summer daycamp building. The remains of an old orchard are to the left. Walking due south, you arrive next at the Mill Master's House, which is currently a private residence. At present, comings and goings are monitored by an orange cat and a

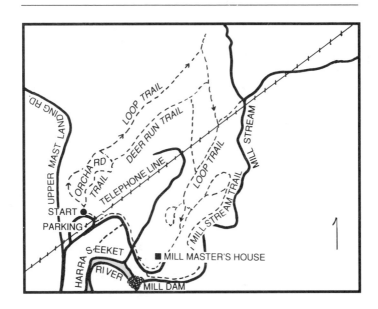

friendly old black dog that may come out to greet you.

Walk down the road from the Mill Master's House to the short side path to the Mill Dam on your left. Here you can watch the Mill Stream as it drops into the lowland known as the Harraseeket River Estuary, which widens to become an important river out by Flying Point Road. The dam is now in disrepair, but it's still an interesting sight— and something of an engineering marvel when you consider how primitive were the means by which these great stone blocks were cut and hauled into place.

Head downhill by the estuary where the road crosses a feeder brook. As the road begins to climb again to the northwest, a side trail departs left to the estuary. (The Estuary Trail makes a loop that also returns to the parking area.) The road crests soon after the Estuary Trail junction, and you arrive, on your right, at the place where you left your car. The entire loop can be completed at a leisurely pace in about an hour and a half. A complete guide to all the trails and natural features of Mast Landing can be purchased at Maine Audubon Society, 118 U.S. Route 1, Falmouth, ME 04105.

13. WOLF NECK WOODS/ FREEPORT

A glance at a map of Maine reveals some striking geographic information. The jagged line of the Maine coast resembles that of Norway. The midcoast region, particularly, embraces a coastline of deeply intruding bays and low mountains that dip abruptly to the waters. This is a coastline of necks, points, and peninsulas that have about them a fjordlike quality. None of the hundreds of inlets that make up the coast actually qualifies for the fjord label (with the exception of Somes Sound on Mount Desert), but still, it's this plenitude of deep bays, inlets, and natural harbors that renders Maine so attractive to the coastal hiker and sailor alike. Wolf Neck, in Freeport, is a narrow point of land running southwest-northeast, bordered

by the Harraseeket River on the west and Casco Bay on the southeast. A network of trails here provides some fine walking along the shores and through the woodlands of this unique coastal terrain.

Wolf Neck Woods, with its surrounding shore zone, is a band of land running across the middle of the peninsula. It is now a Maine state park. The woods were donated for public use in 1969 by the Lawrence Smith family of Freeport and comprise some two hundred acres. The thoughtful gift of the Wolf Neck parklands allows the hiker to tramp through a lovely stretch of superb wooded shore that might otherwise have been off-limits. The trails of the park can be walked in any season and are most attractive in autumn and winter.

To reach Wolf Neck Woods, head east on Dow Street from Freeport center, continuing northeast on Flying Point Road. Two-and-a-quarter miles from Freeport center, bear right on Wolf Neck Road. The road winds southward through a number of small coastal farms and brings you shortly to the well-marked entrance to the park on your left. In high season, the gatehouse is manned and a small fee is charged for entry. Ask the attendant for a park map to orient you.

Wolf Neck is crisscrossed by a half-dozen pleasant trails. The route described here runs around the periphery of the park, with good water views on both sides of the neck. All the trails in the park radiate from a hub at the south end of the main parking area. Many of the walks possible here might be dubbed "self-guiding." With the map in this book and various trail-side markers and legends, you can't get lost, and you will pick up much information about the natural life of the park as you walk. As you will see, environmental points of interest— plant descriptions, geology, forest growth, erosion, and many other subjects— are explained on placards along the walk. This feature makes Wolf Neck an excellent tour for the young. Children can learn here, in an adventuresome way, how to *see* the natural world at work. Gather at the southeast corner of the parking area, and you're ready to start.

Walk southeast and east on the Casco Bay Trail. You'll pass through groves of fine white birch where the ground lies richly carpeted in wood ferns. Soon you bear left and move down some steps over a ledgy area, descending through spruce and fir to the water's edge. A glance to the northeast reveals Googins Island,

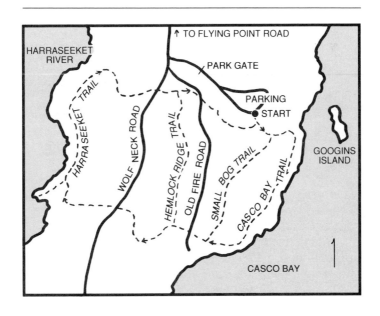

now preserved as an osprey sanctuary. Several of the tall trees on the island have been nesting sites for the birds. Below, you'll see some dramatic examples of the neck's geology. Sedimentary rock, laid down millions of years ago by water deposition, lies exposed here, twisted and upfolded. One can see the work of thousands of years in a few inches of layered rock, now washed clean by the tides.

Proceed southwest along the trail, across a tiny footbridge and through a cluster of young hemlock. At one-half mile you begin to turn inland across the center of the neck. You climb a low hillock into evergreen groves and then level off, walking easily toward the northwest. Passing through a stand of mature pine, you drop down into a depression, cross a fire road, and go under a power line. You soon cross an old stone wall and continue westerly amid attractive white pine, gray birch, red spruce, and hemlock. Bunchberries, their deep green leaves topped by brilliant red berries by late summer, grow along the path. You next pass the Hemlock Ridge Trail coming in on the right. Keep left on what is now the Harraseeket Trail, which continues northwest, and enter another depression after climbing down some ledges. In minutes you cross Wolf Neck Road. Moving past a range of densely grown pines, you approach the water on the west side of the peninsula. As you descend toward the cliffs, watch for a side trail on the left. It runs to some ledgy outlooks with grand views over the river toward South Freeport.

Continue north on the Harraseeket Trail high above the river. Making a circuit above several steep inlets, you turn inland and surmount a rise, pulling around to the southeast. Passing through attractive mature hemlocks, you recross the road. Back in the woods, you momentarily cross a little-used fire road bordered by lowbush blueberries and then proceed southeast again.

This dense woodland was the scene of Colonial outposts in the 1700s. You are not far here from the site of the Means Massacre. In May of 1756, Indians attacked settlers along the point. The Thomas Means (Maens) family, though warned of the Indians' approach, did not proceed immediately to a nearby fortified blockhouse but tarried until the following day. The Indians arrived in the darkness of early morning and shot and scalped Means and one of his children. A daughter was captured and taken to Quebec, while Mrs. Means and two children escaped to the blockhouse. Local stories say that Means's son, who ran the Old Holbrook Tavern in Freeport, later encountered and murdered the Indian who had killed his father. Thomas Means, Sr., was the last white man killed by an Indian in Maine.

Pulling around to the east, you shortly join the Casco Bay Trail again. Turn left at this junction, and in moments you'll be back at the trailhead where you parked. The distance around the loop amounts to less than two miles and makes a leisurely 1½-hour walk.

There is good cross-country skiing here, too. Note that in winter the park gate may be closed. In that case, leave your car off the right-hand side of the road north of the gate and walk into the park. The large sign at the southeast corner of the parking lot has been recently removed, but may be replaced in season with a new marker.

14. Reid State Park/ Georgetown

Georgetown, if one looks closely enough, is an island. A finger of land south of Bath and Woolwich, Georgetown and its neighbor, Arrowsic, are separated from the mainland by a network of streams, rivers, coves, and hidden bays.

The main island is divided from Arrowsic by Back River, while Robinhood Cove and Sagadahoc Bay bisect the hilly land from the north and south. All this land and water interface adds up to some exceptionally beautiful terrain, including what I consider to be the loveliest state park anywhere in New England.

The attractive drive down to Georgetown from U.S. Route 1 in Woolwich will expose you to some of the pretty countryside we've been talking about. From Route 1 on the east side of the Kennebec, turn south on Maine Route 127. You'll cross the Sasanoa and

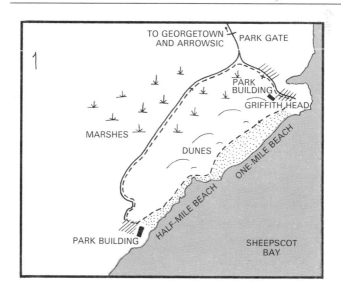

TO GEORGETOWN AND ARROWSIC — PARK GATE — PARK BUILDING — GRIFFITH HEAD — MARSHES — DUNES — ONE-MILE BEACH — HALF-MILE BEACH — PARK BUILDING — SHEEPSCOT BAY

Back rivers and the upper reaches of Robinhood Cove as you travel down through Arrowsic and into Georgetown. Roughly 9½ miles below Woolwich, the road to Reid State Park bears sharply right. Traveling less than three miles on this side road, which runs along Harmon Harbor, will bring you to the park entrance. Keep left shortly and leave your car at the large parking area on your left in about one-quarter mile.

From the parking lot, walk south toward Griffith Head. You pass over a bridge spanning an inlet of Sheepscot Bay, with fine views to the marshes in the southwest and to attractive tidal pools to the northeast. Thick stands of evergreen meet the water's edge. Continue southeast past the park administration building, and east up Griffith Head.

The head, a high pink-granite bluff, furnishes excellent views up and down Sheepscot Bay. The rocky mass immediately to the east is Outer Head, which can be easily reached on foot at low tide. Also to the east are Southport and Cape Newagen. Still farther east, you may be able to see the long north-south line of Damariscove Island.

From Griffith Head, walk down onto One-Mile Beach. This long white strand leads you southward to the park's other extremity. Grass-topped dunes back up to the beach. Ellingwood Rock and Seguin Island are the major offshore landmarks to the south.

A series of ledges are crossed at the end of One-Mile Beach. You turn slightly inland here around the end of the dunes and pass a picnic area. A path takes you farther south onto Half-Mile Beach. Continue south along this more remote sand strip. Wild roses bloom in season where vegetation borders the sand.

Watch for the southern park administration building on your right. Cross a parking area and turn right on a paved road. You wind generally northeast through the great marsh that lies behind the dunes. Gulls soar overhead, and many species of birds feed and nest in the green denseness of the marshland.

In about 2¼ miles, you'll arrive at the junction of the park entrance roads. Bear right at this junction, and it's only a short walk east to your car.

15. JOSEPHINE NEWMAN
SANCTUARY/GEORGETOWN

Named after its donor, the Newman Sanctuary in Georgetown is a 119-acre woodland on a neck of attractive land bounded on two sides by Robinhood Cove. The thickly forested terrain lies on a rib of upfolded, metamorphosed rock, mostly schists and quartzite, laid down in the Devonian period over 300 million years ago.

The sanctuary is home to a rich variety of living things. Maine Audubon's guide to the preserve lists fifty-eight types of wildflowers, grasses, and sedges; thirty-nine shrub species; nineteen different trees;

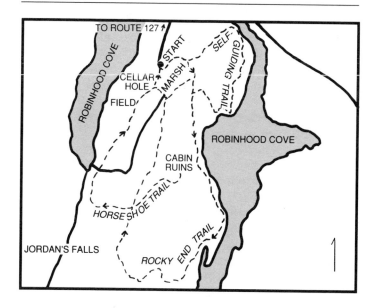

seven species of mosses and lichens; and fourteen species of woodland ferns. A walk through the Newman Sanctuary is a peaceful experience; it is an uncrowded place and a fine example of an ecologically rich Maine coastal woodland.

The sanctuary lies off Maine Route 127 nine miles south of its junction with U.S. Route 1 in Woolwich. The park entry is on the right-hand side of Route 127 on a sharp bend in the road just past the U.S. Post Office in Georgetown. A sign marks the entrance just before the steps to Georgetown Public Library. Head down the entry road slowly; the gravel way is rough and often muddy in places after rains. Park out of the right-of-way in the lot at the end of the road.

Walk south from the parking lot under some big white pines to a signboard at the edge of a pasture. This spot is the hub of the major trails that cover the sanctuary. Turn sharply left here onto the Blue Self-Guiding Trail, which you will follow to the Rocky End Trail, the route you will walk most of the way. The blue-blazed path drops quickly eastward into coniferous woods and past a stone wall. A low, brushy marsh lies to your right. One leg of the Blue Trail shortly runs left (it is part of a loop), but keep right and continue past this junction, going southeast and south until you come to the red-blazed Rocky End Trail on your right. The canopy here is attractive mixed-growth forest, including red and white pine, red oak, white birch, red spruce, and balsam. The big white pines under which you walk directly in this first section of the red-blazed trail have enormous root systems that are visible on the trail's surface for some distance here. You continue south and begin to descend through a grove of spindly, close-grown young balsams intermixed with red spruce. Winterberry holly, wild strawberry, dwarf sarsaparilla, and wild cherry provide groundcover. The Rocky End Trail now drops abruptly to the water's edge at Robinhood Cove. This channel has swiftly moving tidal currents and a six- to eight-foot tidal range. If you happen to pass this way at low tide you'll see exposed mudflats extending toward the main channel. Quahogs, small Macoma, and soft-shelled clams live in the flats. Yellow lichens and some of the mosses common to the sanctuary cover the ledges along the shore. Salt hay and cordgrass grow in marshy pockets.

The trail next runs southeast, staying close to the water amid more balsam and red spruce. At a giant bent pine the route begins to pull away from the shore (just above a small nub of land that juts out into the cove) and climbs sharply by a big, ledgy formation on the right. In this drier ground, beech, oak, and maple supplant the evergreens that characterized the path near the water's edge. Soon you come to the stone wall that marks the southern boundary of the preserve. You turn right and west here, go over a series of ribs, and descend southwest through a stand of balsam. Trailing arbutus, bellwort, meadowsweet, hazelnut, winterberry holly, and starflower are seen at ground level in season.

As you walk more to the north, the trail opens up in stands of big gray birch and red oak. Still on the high ground of the sanctuary, you slowly descend and come to a trail-crossing where you bear left and west onto the orange-blazed Horseshoe Trail. The route now drops to the west through balsam growth while proceeding across two stone walls, one of which then parallels the trail for a short distance. In minutes you come to an old woods road and turn northward again. The old road lies on the right of the stream bed, which is dry much of the year but feeds an arm of Robinhood Cove when running.

Maine Audubon lists thirty-eight bird species that live and breed in the sanctuary and another thirty-one species that are transient here. They range from large birds like the barred owl, pileated woodpecker, great blue heron, and snowy egret, to smaller, familiar ones such as the American goldfinch, red-winged blackbird, black-capped chickadee, and American robin. If you're interested in birding, this walk demands that you carry binoculars with you. Even if you're not a bird expert, this walk is an excellent opportunity to observe and become familiar with avian wildlife.

The last leg of the route continues northward on the Horseshoe Trail in stands of aspen and pine. You enter the low end of a pasture and proceed across it to the signboard at the trailhead. Continue northward past the sign a few paces to your car.

An excellent description of natural features of the Newman Sanctuary and commentary for a self-guiding walk along the blue trail are found in *Forests, Fields and Estuaries,* available from Maine Audubon, 118 U.S. Route 1, Falmouth, ME 04105. (1991 price: $3.50 plus 52¢ postage.)

16. Montsweag Preserve/ Woolwich

Not far north of the growth and bustle of the
Bath-Brunswick area, the Montsweag Preserve is the
site of an interesting, attractive woods walk on a
finger of land pointing down to the Atlantic. The
preserve, owned by The Nature Conservancy, is the
gift of Lois Thurston. It lies not far off U.S. Route 1
between Woolwich and Wiscasset and is easily
reached. Driving north from Bath and Woolwich,
watch for Montsweag Road on your right about one-
half mile south of the Montsweag Farm Restaurant.
The road is marked by a sign on a tree, but you will
need to slow down and watch carefully for it. Go
south on the Montsweag Road for about 1¼ miles

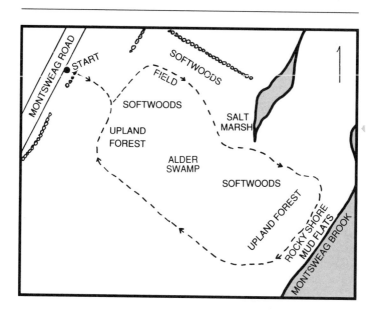

and look very carefully for the trailhead on your left, marked only by a small blue blaze on a tree. It's easy to miss, so watch for power-line pole 56-57. The entrance to the woods is just left of the pole. Park off the road here on the shoulder.

You step down off the road and through a clump of ground juniper into a shady grove of white pine to where a large signboard shows the trail route: a broad

circle that leads off the tableland, through a bog, and to the rocky shore of the inlet on which the preserve fronts. Although the trail is blazed throughout, it does not carry much traffic and is overgrown and brushy in places. It is a good idea to bring a compass on this walk and keep your eyes open for blazes where the groundcover is dense. It's very unlikely, but should you become lost, remember to take a compass reading for west-northwest, and you will eventually come back to the road.

From the trailhead signboard, the route descends slightly to the east and southeast, with a stone wall on the right. Pines yield to scrub oak, and the trail shortly reaches a junction marked by wooden blue arrows on a tree. One can go either way here, but the route described goes left and northeast on a clear path. This is dry, high ground. From here on the trail will gradually work its way to lower ground and the tidal waters of Montsweag Brook.

Having turned left at the arrows, you walk northeastward and soon pass diagonally through a low stone wall. The walk is now slightly uphill in a corridor of stunted white pines that form an attractive cover.

Black-throated green warblers and black-capped chickadees flit between the branches. Watch cautiously for a sharp right turn as you crest a low rise. You turn east and southeast here and march down the right side of a small, open meadow. A blue blaze marks the turn.

The easy descent to the marsh is accomplished in the length of the field. Just before you reach the end of the open ground, the trail re-enters the woods at a white pine on the right. You continue southeast here through a shady pine grove, watching carefully for blazes. In about one hundred yards, the trail pulls to the left and comes to the edge of a marsh by another big pine. The trail markings seem to run out here, so watch carefully. Keeping a few yards right of the big pine, head across the finger of the marsh going due east. You are in the cordgrass and salt hay only a few moments, but there are fine views up the marsh to the north. This part of the trail may be wet at certain times of the year, so wear waterproof foot gear.

Once you've crossed the marsh, look for the remains of an old woods road along which you walk to the east. You'll have to go into the woods thirty yards or so before you'll see the first blaze on a tree to the left. Walking on the level eastward, you come, in about one hundred yards, to a point where the trail leaves this old road and bears sharply left. Oak, beech, and pine cover yields to balsam and hemlock as you come to the water's edge. A small tidal inlet lies to your left as the trail skirts the lichen-covered ledges.

The trail around this little point runs first northeast, then east, and eventually turns to the south. Soon you can see the Chewonki Foundation docks on the far side of the inlet on what is known as Chewonki Neck. A quiet place with occasional boat traffc, the wide channel makes a pretty sight.

A march southward along the water's edge runs through beech groves and then through stands of fir as the trail climbs slowly. A large half-submerged ledge can be seen on the right. Step off the trail to the left here and onto the shore or ledges. There are excellent views down Montsweag Brook to the islets that lie off the point to the south. In high summer on a warm day, settling here on the rocks and eating lunch can be a pleasant experience. If you're interested in the marine biology of the Maine coast, walking along the mudflats here may be possible at low tide.

The trail makes an abrupt turn to the right and northwest at a three-trunked oak on the right *before* you reach a low stone wall. If you come to the wall without seeing the turn, backtrack and look for the tree and blazes on your left. The trail meanders southwest, west, and northwest through mixed growth and over a series of ribs, and then begins to descend to a boggy area by a stone pile that was probably an old foundation. Passing through the boggy slump, the trail heads west through close-grown brush and a grove of white pines. Another low, wet area that carries runoff into Montsweag Bay is below to the left. As you continue farther inland, the trail runs through a brief depression and then climbs slowly to the northwest and north. A side trail departs left to a house near the end of the loop. (Don't miss the blazes on the main trail, or you will end up in the back yard of that house.) Staying on the main trail to northward, you'll arrive, past the house, at the trail junction marked with arrows. Bear left now on the feeder trail and in minutes you're back at the roadside.

The circuit through Montsweag Preserve amounts to just under a 1¼-mile hike and takes 1½ to 2 hours at a moderate pace. Given the attractiveness of the terrain, the water views, and the opportunity to explore the shoreline, hikers should probably budget more than this minimum time to complete the circuit.

Additional information on the preserve and other natural areas in Maine may be found in *Maine Forever—A Guide to Nature Conservancy Preserves in Maine,* available from the Maine Chapter of The Nature Conservancy, 122 Main Street (P.O. Box 338), Topsham, ME 04086.

17. Wiscasset Village

Wiscasset has always been one of those Maine towns you simply can't pass through without stopping. The reasons for scrapping all one's plans, getting out of the car, and exploring the town are plentiful.

The broad and pleasing expanse of the Sheepscot River awaits inspection at the foot of Wiscasset's Main Street. Attractive shops and galleries provide a showcase in the town center for Maine artists and craftsmen. And on the quiet, shady side streets that run north and south from Main, historic houses, churches, museums, and other buildings delight the eye. For the nautically inclined, viewing the two schooner hulks that lie moldering in the river by the town wharf is intriguing. Whether the locals are correct in calling their town the prettiest in Maine, we'll leave to you to

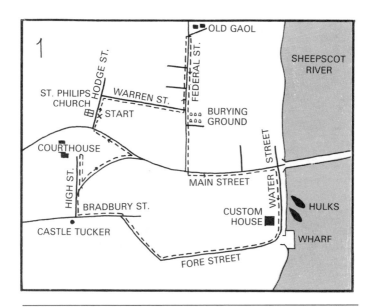

decide. Certainly, as you walk the coast, you'll find much to discover and enjoy in Wiscasset.

From U.S. Route 1, Wiscasset's Main Street, locate Hodge Street where it departs north opposite the Lincoln County Courthouse. Begin your walk by St. Philips Church, an architecturally interesting house of worship constructed in 1822. Walking downhill to the north, you soon bear right onto Warren Street. Here, you'll spot the Maine Art Gallery in what was formerly an old brick academy. Check notices for current exhibitions.

At the bottom of the hill, turn left and walk north on Federal Street past many fine old homes, the most notable of which, Octagon House, was built in 1855 by Captain George Scott. You pass the end of Hooper Street, and the Damon House (1805) is seen on the left a short way beyond. Passing the new grammar school, you turn right on Morton Street. Wiscasset's Old Gaol and Gaoler's House are here, a reminder of the harsh means our forebears used to contain criminality. The jail, built here in 1809 near the site of the original settlement, is formed by forty-one-inch granite blocks. Inside, iron doors and all the grisly stuff of prisons await your inspection. Next door, the Gaoler's House now serves as the Lincoln County Museum.

When you've had your fill of penology, retrace your steps on Federal Street, noting on your left the old burying ground at the corner of Lincoln Street. Its oldest headstone dates from 1739. The man buried beneath the stone, so the legend says, drowned in the Sheepscot when swept from his canoe by an irate bear. The Lincoln County Fire Museum and the Nickels-Sortwell House are soon reached. Both are open to the public in season.

At Main Street, you bear left and walk toward the Sheepscot for two blocks, turning right and south on Water Street. Shortly, on your right, the attractive old Custom House comes into view. Built just after the Civil War, the building once monitored the commerce of a busy port. Opposite the Custom House, a new wharf makes a good spot to look over Wiscasset's hulks, the *Hesper* and the *Luther Little*, both of which have been grounded here since 1932. (The *Luther*

Little still has the stumps of its masts.)

Now, turn right (northwest) and walk up Fore Street to where it connects with Bradbury Street. Continue northwest, watching for the great Georgian structure known as Castle Tucker, opposite the end of High Street. Castle Tucker (1807) was the fourth great house built in Wiscasset by Silas Lee. It is open to visitors in summer and contains Captain Richard Tucker's original furnishings from the 1860s.

Bear right and head up High Street. As you walk northward here, you'll pass the Wood-Foote and Tucker-White houses, the Carleton House, and Lenox House. Carleton House was acquired by shipowner Moses Carleton from its builder, Joseph Wood, in trade "for a hundred puncheons of rum." The Clark-Wood House and the Lee-Smith House (1792) are next in line before the tall-spired Congregational Church. The present church, constructed in this century, is the third built on the site since 1767. The last building on the hill, the Lincoln County Courthouse, dates from 1824 and is the oldest building of its type in Maine where justice is still dispensed on a regular basis.

To complete your walk of the town, simply continue north across Route 1 to Hodge Street and St. Philips Church. The full route described here covers about $2\frac{1}{4}$ miles and can be walked in $1\frac{1}{2}$ hours.

18. BALD MOUNTAIN/
CAMDEN

One of the most attractive mountain walks in the Camden area takes the hiker up Bald Mountain on the west side of Megunticook Lake. Bald Mountain, happily, isn't heavily frequented, as are some of the other main summits in the Camden area. The prospects here are mainly inland over the lakes and hills of east-central Maine, and the slopes of Bald provide an excellent platform for viewing that collection of mountains known as the Camden Hills. This is an excellent mountain to stroll in autumn, spring, and summer, and may be done in winter as well. Snowmobilers sometimes make a trail on the mountain, so the snow is often packed and suitable for hiking even in the cold months.

To reach Bald from U.S. Route 1, head west on Mechanic Street, which leaves the center of the Camden business district opposite Camden National Bank. Follow this street, which becomes a rural road running northwest out of town. When the road first forks, take the right-hand route. At the second fork, bear left and continue until the road ends. Turn left onto Molyneaux Road, and then take the first right (which comes up very quickly) onto Howe Hill Road. Another eight-tenths of a mile brings you to the trailhead, a gravel road on the left by utility pole 18. (If you come to a big farmhouse with a cluster of outbuildings, you have gone too far. Reverse direction and watch for the trail on your right.) Park your car on the shoulder of the road.

With a small, year-round brook to the left, the trail follows a gravel tote road to the south on a brisk grade. The mountain is before you, above and to the right. The road follows the brook through several clearings, pulling around to the southeast and coming shortly to a curve. The trail now passes through the remains of a stone wall, then turns to the northwest through groves of beech, oak, and maple. Leafy and dense in summer, the trail is open, with good visibility, in fall and winter.

The trail follows the tote road farther uphill as the thick, deciduous growth yields to some scattered red spruce, hemlock, and white pine. Some older gray birch are passed, and the trail levels, soon passing a grassy road on the left. Continue straight on toward the northwest. Walking past some giant oaks on your left, you come momentarily to a broad, open clearing. This is a burnt-over blueberry field, so be careful where you walk. Step to the right on the exposed bits of ledge for outstanding views of surrounding hills and, of course, the long expanse of Megunticook Lake.

The route to the top resumes by running behind this open field and heading uphill again to the left and southwest. The ground becomes more brushy here, and the trail begins to move through a series of S-curves that carry you gradually up the steep north

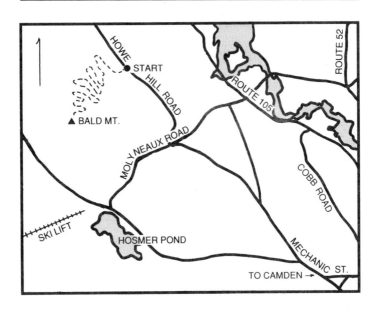

side of the mountain. A long stretch of good-sized beeches dominates this section of the trail. You'll walk through bunches of juniper as the trail runs over sections of exposed ledge in spruce, aspen, and white birch. The ground may be wet here with funneled runoff. Passing an open, ledgy area just below the top, you emerge quickly on the bald, stony summit about 1½ miles above the paved road.

The views from up here are as good as any in the Camden Hills, and all the better because so little of the man-made world is visible from this spot. The most obvious sights are the major hills of the Camden range opposite to the east and northeast. Directly across Megunticook Lake is the rock wall of Maiden Cliff. Above it is Zeke's Lookout and, to the right, the broad shoulder of Mount Megunticook, the highest summit in the Camden Hills. The slightly lower hump of Cameron Mountain is just behind and to the left of Maiden Cliff. The hills of Knox and Waldo counties are off to the northwest, while views to the ocean are east and south. The ragged arm of land projecting into Megunticook Lake is Fernald's Neck (described in the next chapter.) North of Megunticook are the connected Norton and Coleman ponds. And, as noted, the views here are all the sweeter for so little evidence of man's intrusion.

The walk to the summit of Bald Mountain takes about 1¼ hours— slightly longer in winter, when it is possible to snowshoe most of the way. Walkers should note that a number of old woods roads intersect the main road and trail at various points. Stay with the blue-blazed route all the way to the summit.

19. FERNALD'S NECK PRESERVE/CAMDEN & LINCOLNVILLE

Fernald's Neck in Camden and Lincolnville is a place of superlatives. This beautiful 315-acre preserve, lying at the center of Megunticook Lake in both Knox and Waldo counties, protects eighteen thousand feet of pristine shore in the heart of the Camden Hills. Nathaniel Fernald came to this point of land in 1806, and Fernald family members have been associated with this territory as farmers and woodcutters ever since.

The peninsula has been used for pasture, bisected by stone walls, heavily logged, and otherwise cultivated by man, but in the last fifty years it has largely reverted to its natural state. Although housing developers sought to forever alter this ground for commercial purposes, local people banded together in 1969 to buy the neck, donating it to the Maine Chapter of The Nature Conservancy, its current owners. Fernald's Neck Preserve is today a superb, densely wooded tramping ground for hikers, birdwatchers, and those interested in the plant and animal life of midcoast Maine.

To walk Fernald's Neck, drive west on Maine Route 52 from U.S. Route 1 in Camden center toward Lincolnville. Passing the lake on your left, you come to a Y in the road known as Young's Corner (Youngtown). Keep left on Route 52 here and, making the bend, come immediately to a side road on your left opposite green highway marker number 5016. Turn left (southwest) on this side road, which runs between some cottages on the northeast side of Megunticook Lake. Shortly the road divides, and you keep left again on a gravel track marked by a small Nature Conservancy sign. Follow this track south (leave your car out on the pavement if you visit in mud season, as this section can be boggy), climbing to a farmhouse, which you skirt around in about one-quarter mile. A grassy parking area lies past a second old house in a high pasture with splendid views toward Maiden Cliff. Park here, being careful not to block the entry.

The walk follows an obvious path downhill through the hayfield to the south and southwest, where it enters the woods at a crumbling stone wall. The entrance is marked by a Nature Conservancy signboard. The route continues southwest through a fragrant corridor of densely grown hemlock. Occasional views open up leftward to the shores of the lake. The walking is wet in places as you pull around to the south and then climb slightly to a splendid grove of towering hemlocks. Going through another stone wall, you arrive shortly at a trail junction marked by a signboard and trail register. An old logging ramp lies in the brush to the left. A pamphlet, "Fernald's Neck Preserve Guide," is available here, and walkers should sign-in on the trail register. Make sure the register box is latched against the weather before you move on.

From this clearing depart two major loops that cover the upper and lower sections of the neck. We'll walk the upper loop on the blue and red trails. Start by keeping right at the trail register and heading west over level ground amid big pines and hemlocks. The trail drops southwest through a wet depression, coming soon to another junction. Go straight ahead (left) here on the blue trail, traveling over more damp ground, spongy with sphagnum and haircap mosses. Decaying, fallen hemlock in the brush is spotted with *Ganoderma tsuga,* a shelf fungus. Passing two old maples, you next descend southward among more hemlock and balsams, soon noting the yellow trail, which comes in from the left. Continue on the blue trail, dropping to a gully grown up with wood ferns. This is good cover for game birds, and I have flushed pheasants from the brush here on several occasions.

To your left in this section is the Great Bog, a dense lowland that dominates the center of the neck.

A variety of marsh grasses and rushes can be found here. Blue flag iris, pitcher plant, and rose pogonia thrive, along with pipewort, arrowhead, bur-reed, pondweed, and bulrushes. Rhodora, sweet gale, and leatherleaf prosper along the edge of the bog. Wood ducks, Canada geese, and black ducks have been seen nesting in the area, too.

Walk now through a clutch of boulders, through a stand of silver birch, and uphill among still more boulders. The yellow trail leaves to the right in this

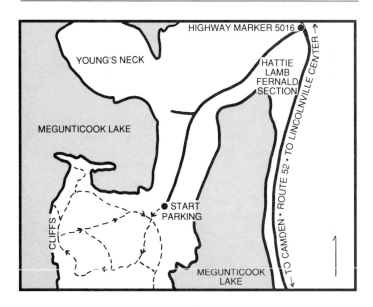

section. Over a rocky hump, you drop to the edge of the bog and come shortly to the border of the preserve. The trail makes an abrupt uphill turn to the north here, meandering over several ledgy ribs in groves of highly attractive hemlock and red and white pine. The terrain here is so extravagantly perfect that it's hard to believe this land was ever logged or otherwise commercially exploited. In just a few minutes, the trail rises to open cliffs that overlook the west side of Megunticook Lake. The views from the cliffs are as fine as the woodlands you just walked through, and one can see birdlife along the shore far below. The prospect over some of the surrounding mountains is good here, too.

The trail continues northward over a series of ledges marked by fallen logs and thick growths of lichen. White and red pine, ground juniper, and hemlock dot the ledges. Dropping down, you come soon to the red trail on your right, which runs east at a sharp angle. Make the turn onto the red trail, walking past some large boulders, deposited here as glacial erratics. Continuing eastward, pass a stagnant pond. Several trees in this section are full of holes, witness to the labors of the pileated woodpecker.

Momentarily, you pass the other end of the yellow trail, which appears to the right. The route now drops northeastward through lovely hemlock stands, some of which crowd the path. When the blue trail rejoins the red trail, keep right and walk eastward to the trail register. From the register, bear left and return to the field where your walk began. Just before you reach the stone wall and the field, watch for an unmarked path on your right. This unmaintained path circles to the edge of the water, offering excellent views down the channel on the west side of the preserve. It's only a five-minute detour and worth the trouble. Returning to the main trail, continue northeast to the field and parking area.

20. Mount Megunticook & Mount Battie/ Camden

Camden has long been a favorite spot for Maine shore visitors. No wonder; situated right in the middle of the Maine coast, the town boasts a superb harbor, stately old homes, interesting shops, an attractive state park, and a group of elegant little mountains. Whether you like messing about the shore or taking to the woods and hills, there's something to do in Camden, always against a fine backdrop of sea and highlands.

One of the best ways to get acquainted with Camden and the part of the Penobscot Bay coast on which it fronts is to head for the highlands encircling the town. Nine summits of varying height form an arc south, west, and north of Camden village; most of these lie within Camden Hills State Park. In addition to the three routes in the Camden area described in this book, other pathways are shown in the Appalachian Mountain Club's Camden Hills map available in some local stores. (See also the author's *50 Hikes in Southern Maine,* Backcountry Publications, 1989, for further walks in the Camden region.)

Mount Megunticook is a low, sprawling mountain that dominates the Camden Hills range and is the highest of the summits. The mountain will challenge the walker with a good long march over it and its neighbor, Mount Battie, with splendid views of the ocean to eastward. To walk this circuit, drive north from Camden center on U.S. Route 1, turning left into Camden Hills State Park 2¾ miles from town. A fee is charged for entry to the park in summer, but you can usually park free of charge in a small, grassy field to

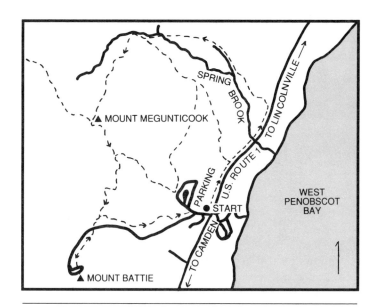

the left and just in front of the gatehouse, if you're
just going to hike and don't intend to camp or drive
up the Mount Battie auto road. A good map of the
park may be available at the gate in season.

Leaving your car here by the gate, walk back to
U.S. Route 1 and follow its left side north on the
shoulder for about one mile. Watch for the trailhead,
which is grassy and overgrown, lying between two
houses. A small sign that used to mark the trailhead
has recently been removed, the trail dropped from the
state park's trail map, and the route left to grow wild.
The trailhead is opposite telephone pole 85-15, and
can still be found easily, despite these ill-considered
changes. Leave the road here and walk west on what,
for many years, was the Spring Brook Trail, and is
still so identified on older maps, such as one from the
Appalachian Mountain Club. The path runs through
tall grasses and dips into the woods, following the
watercourse of the same name up an old logging
road. Continue west of this disused woods road for
1½ miles, where you intersect the Slope Trail. Turn
left on the Slope Trail just east of the old ski shelter.

Once on the Slope Trail, you climb directly south-

westward toward the true summit of Mount Megunticook, ascending gradually over easy grades through
attractive mixed growth. Passing through a short
eroded stretch, you reach the Ridge Trail at just
under three miles from the road. The best views will
lie just east of this wooded spot. Turn left and descend slightly eastward for about one-third of a mile
to Ocean Lookout. Here you'll find the superb views
mentioned earlier. Bald Rock and Garey mountains

lie to the north. The long, thin expanse of Islesboro
runs north and south in the Atlantic off to the northeast. North Haven and Vinalhaven are well offshore to
the southeast. Due east, and visible only on a clear
day, is the distinctive shape of Deer Isle. The lookout
provides the best vantage point in Camden for sur-
veying Penobscot Bay.

You next walk the Tableland Trail toward Mount
Battie off to the southeast. The path descends steeply
to the left of two series of ledges and then pulls
around toward the southwest, descending more gradually through several S-curves before emerging on the
Mount Battie auto road, about 1¼ miles below the
lookout. Cross Mount Battie Road, climbing gradually

to the southwest and south, arriving in one-half mile at the Mount Battie parking area.

The views of Camden from Mount Battie's stone tower are particularly good. The harbor, which is home to Maine's windjammer fleet, lies to the southeast, roughly bounded by Northeast Point and Dillingham Point. Around to the south, you can glimpse Rockport. Further out to the east-southeast, Isle au Haut may be seen over North Haven and Vinalhaven if the weather is clear.

To complete this walk, retrace your steps on the Tableland Trail until you come to the Mount Battie Road. Cross the road and watch for another trail that runs off Tableland to the right just a few hundred yards into the brush. Bear right on the Nature Trail and follow it east for about one mile as it descends to the park gate where you left your car.

This entire loop of over six miles can be completed in 4$\frac{1}{2}$ hours of brisk walking. Allow more time for rest and lunch on Ocean Outlook or the summit of Mount Battie.

21. CASTINE VILLAGE

The lovely coastal town of Castine occupies an irregular peninsula on the east side of Penobscot Bay, opposite Belfast and south of Bucksport. Castine can lay claim to a most unusual history, beginning with its establishment as a French trading post named Pentagoet in 1614. Before the area became fully "American," it passed through the hands of the British and Dutch as well.

Castine may be reached by driving south from U.S. Route 1 in Orland, then following Maine Routes 175 and 166 into the village. On your right, as you head down the peninsula, you'll enjoy some splendid

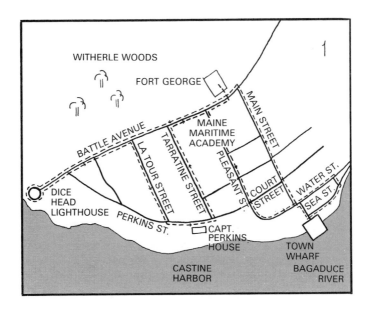

views of upper Penobscot Bay. Just north of the village, you cross the canal built by the British during the War of 1812, which linked Wadsworth Cove and Hatch Cove. As you enter the village, Route 166 shortly becomes Battle Avenue, and Fort George lies on the right.

Because it dominates both the eastern half of Penobscot Bay and the entrance to the Bagaduce River, Castine was a natural site for Colonial fortifications. Fort George, where our walk begins, was built in 1779 by a British detachment under General MacLean. The earthen ramparts of the fort still stand and are interesting to explore. The southwest corner of the fort contains the powder magazine, which was reconstructed in 1962.

Massachusetts launched an attack against the British garrison at Castine in August 1779, with thirty-seven ships and two thousand men. Nine British ships and a few hundred troops routed the ill-fated Penobscot Expedition. Later, Fort George was the last outpost given up by the British at the end of the Revolutionary War. During the War of 1812, the British again occupied Castine and rebuilt the fortifications. They blew up the fort and departed forever in April 1815.

From Fort George, walk south on Pleasant Street, through the buildings of Maine Maritime Academy. The academy, an institution of the state of Maine, provides college-level training to young men and women for seagoing careers. On your right, as you head down Pleasant Street, watch for signs indicating the Allie Ryan Marine Collection, which is open to the public.

At the foot of Pleasant, turn left on Water Street. Before you, if it is in home port, will be the *State of Maine,* a 533-foot training vessel operated by the Maine Maritime Academy. Castine Harbor is the broad expanse of water to the south. Hospital Point and Smith Cove are to the southeast.

Walk east on Water Street through the small commercial section of the town. The town wharf lies down to the right at the foot of Main Street and provides a good vantage point on the harbor. Continuing east on Water Street, take your first right and walk south to Sea Street. Here, good views of the harbor's small-boat fleet may be had. Oakum Bay is to the left.

Following Sea Street southwest, proceed along the waterfront and come back to Maine Street, turning northwest.

Main Street contains several attractive small shops and galleries. The old brick buildings at the foot of Main Street date from the War of 1821. The fine old Pentagoet and Castine inns are on your left and right, respectively, as you head up the hill. Many excellent federal-period homes line the street. As you cross Court Street, look to your right for a glimpse of the Unitarian Church (First Congregational Society), with its Bulfinch-inspired steeple. Built in 1790, the structure contains a bell from the Revere foundry.

At the junction of Main Street and Battle Avenue, walk southwesterly. The stroll to Dice Head is less than a mile. The way features several historic markers explaining military affairs conducted in the area as British, French, Dutch, and American forces contended for the strategic lands of Castine. Near the end of Battle Avenue you reach the old lighthouse at Dice Head.

Returning northeast along Battle Avenue, walk south (right) on La Tour Street and left on Perkins Street. The Wilson Museum stands here, as does the Captain John Perkins House, perhaps the only pre-Revolutionary home remaining in the town. Continuing eastward, walk left up Tarratine Street to Battle and then right to your starting place at Fort George. This walk around Castine village covers about 2½ miles and makes a particularly enjoyable walk in autumn or after a fresh snowfall in winter.

22. BLUE HILL

As you travel northeast along U.S. Route 1 between Bucksport and Ellsworth, one of the most striking sights is the dome-shaped mass of Blue Hill several miles to the south. Blue Hill rises nearly one thousand feet over the harbor and Blue Hill Bay to the southeast and provides excellent outlooks toward Mount Desert Island and south toward Sedgwick and Brooklin.

The trail for Blue Hill is easily located by heading

south on Maine Route 15 from U.S. Route 1 in Orland. Eleven miles south of Route 1, watch for a narrow paved road that turns northeast toward the Blue Hill Fairgrounds. Bear left on this road, which climbs a ridge north of Blue Hill village. Soon you will pass a farmhouse on the left, and a short way beyond it you will reach the signs for the trail to the summit fire tower. Park off the road near the trailhead.

The trail runs nearly due north along a rough jeep track. You can see the summit ledges high up

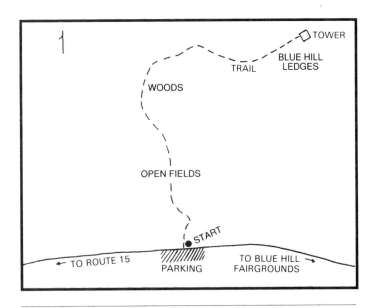

ahead. Walking through young hardwoods, you shortly bear around to the northwest and begin to climb more rapidly.

Turning to the right again toward the north and northeast, you move through dense spruce stands that cap the mountain. Coming out from under the trees, you soon emerge on the open ledge occupied by the Maine Forest Service fire tower.

From the summit of Blue Hill, views take in Chandler Parker Mountain to the west and Brooksville to the southwest. Sedgwick and Brooklin lie more to the south. Long Island makes the largest landmass in upper Blue Hill Bay. Swan's Island lies farther southeast, where the bay becomes the Atlantic. Eastward, you'll see the splendid expanse of Mount Desert Island with its range of mountains running southwest to northeast. North of the hill lie several lakes. The closest is long, slender Toddy Pond in Surry.

The walk up to Blue Hill's summit and back can be done comfortably in 1½ hours. You may want to budget additional time for a stroll through attractive Blue Hill village, just one mile south on Route 15.

23. CROCKETT COVE WOODS
PRESERVE/STONINGTON

Deer Isle is one of the waterbound gems of Penobscot Bay. It's a big island, connected to the mainland by a graceful suspension bridge over Eggemoggin Reach. The island is home to fishermen, lobstermen, artisans, and artists. One of the country's best craft schools— the Haystack School— is on Deer Isle. The two major towns on the island are Deer Isle and Stonington. The latter is a perfect example of a community that depends almost entirely on the sea for its livelihood. Stonington is also the departure point for the ferry to Isle au Haut. Between Deer Isle township and Stonington are rural roads and woodlands that have, so far, escaped the madness of development that constantly pursues the coast of Maine.

　　In one of the prettiest of these undeveloped spots
lies Crockett Cove Woods, a small and very interesting natural area above Crockett Cove on the southwest corner of Deer Isle. The preserve was donated to
The Nature Conservancy by architect and artist Emily
Muir, of Stonington, in 1975. About one hundred
acres in size, Crockett Cove Woods is what The
Nature Conservancy calls "a coastal fog forest"; situated as it is, it collects the winds and weather of
Penobscot Bay. Although this place makes a worth-
while destination for the walker any time, the preserve managers suggest that Crockett Cove Woods
actually is best visited on a foggy, wet day.

　　This fine section of Maine coast is reached by
driving south from U.S. Route 1 in Orland on Maine
Route 15. In Deer Island township, bear right and

south on an unnumbered road to Sunset. Passing through Sunset, watch for Whitman Road about 2½ miles south of the Sunset post office. (If you come north to this point from Stonington, Whitman Road is on your left approximately two miles north of town.) Turn west on Whitman Road, which follows the edge of Burnt Cove, soon dipping right and into the woods. Go through a gate and watch for the trailhead and parking spaces immediately on your right.

Sign in at the trail register by the parking area and pick up a brochure that describes the trail system and includes a map of the preserve. Four trails of varying lengths are available to the walker. I suggest you begin by walking the very short Nature Trail, a self-guiding path that runs northwest from the trail register. Nineteen guideposts along this path are referenced and explained in the brochure noted above. Walking the Nature Trail (an especially good instructional experience for kids over five), you'll get an intimate introduction to the forest trees, groundcover, and bird and animal life that flourish here.

When you reach the end of the short nature walk, retrace your steps, watching for the Loop Trail on

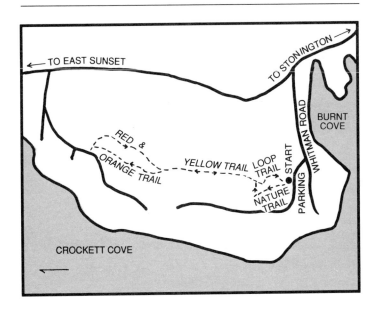

your left. Take it and then bear left and north on the yellow-blazed hiking trail. This is a longer route through the heart of the preserve. This trail carries the walker through a cedar forest, through mixed deciduous and coniferous woods, along a brook that it crosses and recrosses, and beneath big stands of spruce. Closer to the northern end of the preserve you will reach the orange blazes of the Red-Orange Trail. You can go either way at this junction, as this is another loop that will bring you back to the Yellow Trail on your return.

One of the most striking features of Crockett Cove Woods is the lush, moisture-dependent plant life that seems to burgeon everywhere. Witherod, cinnamon fern, bracken fern, creeping snowberry, bunchberry, pitcher plants, Indian pipe, sheep laurel, mountain holly, and large and small cranberry are found in the woods. Red and white spruce, black alder, striped and red maple, tamarack, and cedar line the trails, and the observant naturalist will also find whorled wood aster, red trillium, baneberry, round-leaved sundew, goldthread, twinflower, and bluebead lily. Beard lichens hang from many trees, and rock tripe and reindeer lichen cover most of the boulders and ledges in the preserve. Visitors wanting to familiarize themselves with these various species will find most of them described in the brochure that guides the nature walk.

Red squirrels are the most commonly seen animals in Crockett Woods. Snowshoe hare, the ubiquitous striped skunk, weasel, white-tailed deer, deer mice, raccoons, and masked shrews are also present. How many you see depends upon how quietly and how carefully you walk.

Visitors to the preserve are asked to stay on the trails. Climbing on rocks and through dense, wet groundcover can do much ecological damage. All shrubs, plants, and mosses should, similarly, be left undisturbed for future visitors to see and enjoy.

24. Blagden Preserve at Indian Point/ Mount Desert Island

Most visitors to Mount Desert Island will see the eastern regions of the island that were burnt over in the tragic fires of 1947. But western parts of the island, such as Indian Point, are more interesting for the walker, for here one gets a glimpse of Mount Desert as it once was— thickly forested in coniferous growth attractively intermixed with old hardwoods. One of the costs of a major forest fire is destruction of low-level groundcover. At Indian Point, the walker finds the rich ground canopy of grasses, lichens, and club mosses that are characteristic of the moist, undisturbed forests of north coastal Maine.

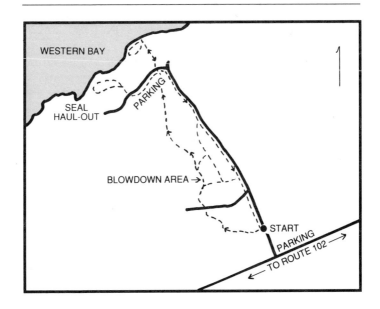

WESTERN BAY

SEAL HAUL-OUT

PARKING

BLOWDOWN AREA →

START
PARKING
TO ROUTE 102 →

In 1968, Donald and Zelina Blagden donated a large parcel of prime Indian Point land to The Nature Conservancy. Now known as the Blagden Preserve, the grounds provide delightful walking for those interested in an unspoiled version of Mount Desert and in fine outlooks on the island's northwest shore. A walk of about 2½ miles can be made within the preserve, which is open to visitors year-round. And because it is in a less-traveled corner of Mount Desert Island, the Blagden Preserve may just be one of the island's most quiet, peaceful places to walk.

Driving to the Blagden Preserve, turn right off Maine Route 3 at the first junction on Mount Desert Island, opposite a filling station. Follow Maine Route 102 and Maine Route 198 in the direction of Somesville. Just under two miles along Route 102, bear right again on Indian Point Road. Follow this road for just over 1¾ miles to the preserve entrance on your right. Park in the grassy lot just inside on the right. A large sign marks the preserve grounds, and it is not difficult to find.

Once arrived, walk up the road and register at the caretaker's cottage. A descriptive map of the preserve is available here. The walk is begun by heading northwest up the paved road, watching for the Big Woods Trail on your left a short way above the cottage. Head west and northwest on this trail over level ground amid a stand of birches. The walk here is shaded by hemlock and red spruce, their shallow roots forming a network over the ground. Beard lichens, which thrive on the moist, balsam-scented air, cling to nearby trees. Continuing through tall spruce and hemlock, the trail zigzags northwestward. Haircap and sphagnum mosses are all about, covering the ground with their intense, textured green. You will pass a clump of blow-downs. Views ahead over the brush toward the bay open up briefly. Occasional white pines begin to interrupt the red spruce canopy. In minutes you will come to a gravel road.

Proceed left a short distance on the road and then bear *right* into the woods as the trail resumes over boggy ground and corduroy platforms. More blow-downs appear, and the trail reaches a junction in a

few minutes. Keep left here and continue northwest and north, descending through somewhat more open woods, coming soon to another connector trail on the right. You proceed straight ahead and momentarily pass through a grove of cedars. The ground becomes boggy again as you walk through more spruces and then across a clearing. Alder, cedar, and hackmatack grow along this trail as it eventually becomes an open, grassy road that you follow to an orchard and the paved road.

Cross the paved road at its bend and follow the path along a fence toward the shore. This little path, which descends to the ledges, is known as the Fern Trail. Coming out onto the rocks, you have superb views up and down Western Bay. The ground you walk on here is very old. Laid down at least 450 million years ago, the striped ledge that predominates here is known as Ellsworth schist. Many of the other boulders that dot the shoreline are products of glacial movement from higher ground inland.

If you walk along the ledges to the west, you'll come to a small, indented beach. The preserve is about a thousand feet wide along the shore, and at its extreme western end are outlooks over offshore ledges often populated by harbor seals. These creatures are year-round residents of the waters surrounding Mount Desert. Please be careful not to stray onto private property at the western end of the preserve shore.

To return to your car, retrace your steps off the beach and along the Fern Trail back to the paved road. Here you may walk back through the forest on the Big Woods Trail again, or follow the paved road for a brisk uphill walk to the caretaker's cottage and the parking area. Allowing time for shore exploration, this hike takes about 2½ hours, slightly less if you return by the road.

Winter hikers are welcome in the park, but it is advisable to call ahead to determine whether the trails are open. Ring up the caretaker at (207) 288-4838. For the dedicated birdwatcher, lists of species commonly seen in the preserve are available at the caretaker's cottage. Please stay on marked trails or on the paved road while in the preserve, respecting the preserve boundaries.

25. SHIP HARBOR NATURE TRAIL/ MOUNT DESERT ISLAND

Few visitors to Mount Desert Island bother to walk in the island's extreme southwest quarter. That is a shame, because this area of Mount Desert is far away from the troublesome crowds that frequent other parts of the island in the high season. The Acadia National Park lands that lie between Southwest Harbor and Bass Harbor along Maine Route 102A are pretty and wild, with diverse terrain and vegetation. Additionally, for those who don't take to mountain climbing, there are easy woods walks along the Atlantic shore in settings that are as beautiful as any found between Maine and Florida.

The Ship Harbor Nature Trail is a self-guiding nature walk along the banks of an almost perfect, protected harbor in a wooded section of parkland on

the coast road south of Southwest Harbor. Along this trail the Park Service has established markers that are keyed to a nature pamphlet usually available at the trailhead or at park headquarters. The route described here varies slightly from the pamphlet description, but the two are complementary. To reach the trailhead for this walk, drive southeast on Maine Route 102A from its junction with Maine Route 102 just south of the Southwest Harbor town center. Follow the road through some staggeringly beautiful coastal terrain and across a natural seawall. Four-and-a-quarter miles south of the junction noted above, watch for a parking area on your left. Leave your car here by a big trail sign.

This walk follows a figure-eight route through the woods. You begin by heading southeast and dipping down into a little hollow grown up with spruce and alder. The harbor, not yet visible, lies to the right, and the sound of shorebirds, busy on the water, is usually audible here. Raspberry bushes grow wild, and bearded lichens hang from some of the weathered old spruce trees. A junction comes up shortly, and you keep left here across some dampish ground and past a pair of gray birches.

The walk next runs through a corridor of attractive,

tall spruce, with a boggy area on the left. The path pulls more to the southeast as this cathedral-like corridor continues, the ground thick with club moss, lichens, and bunchberry. Pass over a ledgy hummock that is more in the open, and then continue in a southwesterly direction to a stately grove along the water's edge. The heart of the fine, protected harbor is to your right. At this point you are at the crux of the figure eight.

Just beyond a post, bear right and follow the path above the harbor and to the *southwest.* The harbor views are excellent here. The trail soon bears to the left and south, running along the edge of the channel. Rocks and roots demand that you pay attention to your footing, particularly on wet days. Below are ledges of the pink granite common to Mount Desert, and there are numerous opportunities to descend to the shore— but use caution. The trail arrives momentarily at an open headland with fine views to Great Gott Island to the south. This makes a good spot to rest and picnic.

At the high end of the figure eight, the trail works around to the left through patches of ground juniper

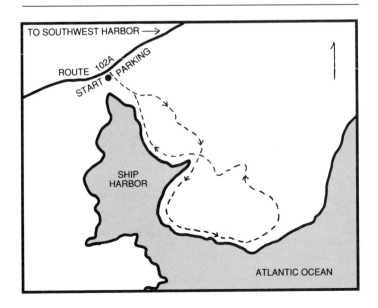

and enters a more open area dotted with hack-matack, or eastern larch, as it is sometimes called. In autumn, these trees turn a golden brown color before dropping their needles. The hackmatack, though a conifer, is deciduous and not a true "evergreen." Going more or less northward now, the trail winds over bare ledges covered with map lichens. Some of these ledges bear the marks of glacial scouring, which has left distinctive grooves in the rock's surface. In minutes, you arrive again at the crux of the figure eight and proceed *northwest*. The trail now follows the shore again, continuing northwesterly over roots and stony ground. One can see left back down the channel to the ocean from here. Walk through scattered balsam and ground juniper to a rocky hump that provides an excellent outlook to the inner limits of the harbor. Many aquatic birds congregate here, particularly ringnecks and buffleheads. The trail now dips through some blow-down, and then climbs past several large birches, coming again to the junction you passed near the beginning of the hike. Go left and north here, and you will emerge shortly at the parking area.

The entire walk along Ship Harbor is 1⅓ miles and can be done in a leisurely hour-and-a-half, but the beauty of the shoreline and the abundance of wildlife here may make you want to spend a good deal longer.

26. Dorr Mountain & Cadillac Mountain/ Mount Desert Island

Mount Desert Island contains Maine's only national park. When you have only one of a thing, it ought to be the very best, and Acadia National Park offers its fair share of superlatives. Southwest Harbor, Cadillac Mountain, Bar Harbor, Frenchman Bay— these names all belong to one of the most attractive areas in all of Maine's great shoreline. Rivaled only by Camden in its unusual mixture of mountains, lakes, and harbors, Mount Desert provides a wealth of fine hiking.

The beauty of Mount Desert and Acadia is a poorly kept secret. Like a great magnet, the island draws visitors in summer swarms. You'll enjoy walking in the park more in spring and autumn, when visitors are fewer and the island is every bit as lovely. Several National Park Service camp-grounds and about a dozen privately owned camping areas offer outdoor accommodations, and motels and hotels are numerous both in Bar Harbor and around nearby Ellsworth on the mainland. Acadia National Park headquarters is at Hulls Cove, Route 3, Bar Harbor, ME 04609. The park phone is (207) 288-3338.

For this coastal walk, we head up two of Mount Desert's highest mountains. Dorr Mountain, which is the third highest summit in Acadia, will be our first objective. From park headquarters, continue along Maine Route 3 through Bar Harbor. Drive southwest out of Bar Harbor, still on Route 3, and pass the Jackson Laboratories on your left. Shortly, turn right

and park at Sieur de Monts Spring.

From the spring, take the Dorr Mountain Trail southwest. You shortly turn northwesterly and then south on a switchback as you move quickly up through young hardwoods. The trail continues south over a series of stone steps. At just over one mile, another switchback takes you northwest. You then follow a series of steep S-curves generally west to the 1,270-foot summit. The views from Dorr's bald, ledgy top are excellent to the north, east, and south. Due east are Huguenot Head and, just to the right, Champlain Mountain. Kebo Mountain lies northward, and the low drainage area of Otter Creek is to the south.

Turn north on the North Ridge Trail and, very shortly, left (west) on the Notch Trail. You quickly descend about two hundred feet into the notch between

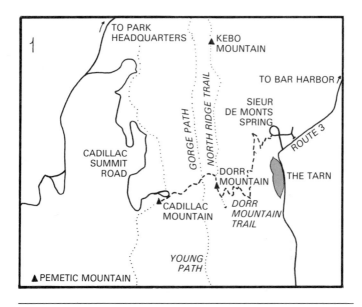

Dorr and Cadillac. You'll reach the Gorge Path and the A. Murray Young Path in one-third of a mile. Continue west and southwest on the Gorge Path, making the steep half-mile ascent of the east face of Cadillac Mountain.

Views from Cadillac's broad summit include those seen from Dorr, but are superior. The Porcupine Islands of Bar Harbor lie to the northeast. Across Frenchman Bay to the east you'll see Schoodic Point, and to the north-northeast Schoodic Mountain (both described elsewhere in this book). Major summits running to the southwest are Pemetic, Penobscot, and Norumbega mountains.

On the return to Sieur de Monts, descend by the same route, using particular care on the east side of Cadillac and Dorr. The round trip takes in 4¾ miles of strenuous walking. Be sure to bring along a park map (available at headquarters) on this walk.

(For other climbs on Mount Desert Island, see *50 Hikes in Southern Maine,* by the same author.)

27.Schoodic Mountain/ East Franklin

Above Frenchman Bay is a series of smaller bays, harbors, and lakes. Overlooking this broad circuit of waterways, Schoodic Mountain in Township 9SD provides a challenging hike of nearly six miles through fine upland woods and over open ledges to a summit with commanding views of Maine's northern coast. At slightly over one thousand feet in elevation, Schoodic Mountain isn't Everest, but its excellent location rewards the walker with fine views of Cadillac Mountain and the other major peaks in Acadia National Park, and also of the inland mountains of the Tunk Lake area. A walk up Schoodic Mountain restores one's perspective, too. Traveling only along the often busy coastline, one tends to forget that most of this corner of Maine (eastern Hancock and Washington counties) is largely unsettled. Schoodic Mountain lies well back in remote, sparsely settled ground, within sight of the coast yet very different in flavor.

The old trail that approached the mountain from the east is now discontinued, and a more direct route from the west is preferred. To reach the mountain, drive north from U.S. Route 1 in Sullivan on Maine Route 200. Follow this side road to East Franklin. About 3¾ miles from Route 1, you will come to two bridges across brooks that feed a nearby marsh. There is room to park north of the second bridge.

The path up Schoodic Mountain begins between the two bridges and runs briefly east up a sharp rise and then levels off. The terrain here is open and dotted with blueberry fields. The walker can see ahead now, toward the summit. The path joins a gravel road and stays with this road as it gradually pulls away from the fields, crosses a brook, and runs through a mixed-growth forest of oak, white birch, red spruce, and beech. Canada mayflower, partridgeberry, and shrubby cinquefoil grow along the trail.

A mile from the road, you arrive at the Maine Central Railroad track. The trail passes through a clutch of rhodora (a heath plant), crosses the railroad track, and then runs east and right again among sarsaparilla and wintergreen. Interrupted and bracken

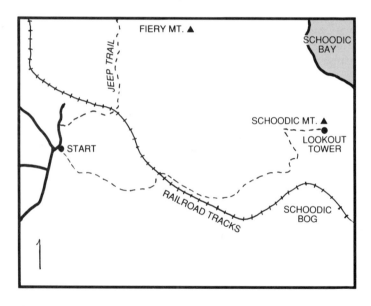

ferns are common in this section. You next begin to pull away from the tracks, marching left and up the grade in the direction of the warden's cabin site. Several tote roads drift off in various directions in the next half-mile; keep left at these forks.

Nearly a mile above the railroad tracks, views begin to open up to the ledges ahead as you continue northeastward, crossing another small brook. Shortly the trail leaves the road, bearing left and uphill again to the site of the former warden's cabin, now in ruins. Turn left here and walk up the steep ledges through open scrub to the col that separates Schoodic Nubble (to the left) and Schoodic's main summit to the east. The grade eases here as you bear right and pass a cairn, following painted blazes on the ledge. There are signs that this mountain was burnt over many years ago. Golden heather, wild blueberry, and ground juniper grow among the lichens that cling to the rock. Small, stunted birches and aspen grow scattered about, able to make a toehold in this windswept, unprotected place. A few more minutes of walking bring you to the summit of Schoodic near the radio tower.

Flanders Pond and Flanders Bay lie to the south as seen from your perch. The great body of water to the east of Mount Desert is Frenchman Bay, with its distinctive collection of islands. Far to the southwest over Hog Bay, you'll spot Blue Hill and the Blue Hill peninsula. The Narraguagus watershed, Donnel Pond, and Lead Mountain are northward. If you look around to the northeast, you will see low mountains: Tunk, Caribou, and Black Cat (with its three distinctive summits). The little summit to the immediate northwest is Fiery Mountain.

The 3½-hour round trip to the top of Schoodic can be done at any time of year, and in winter it is possible to cross-country ski or snowshoe a good part of the route. Probably the best times to walk here are spring or autumn, when the absence of foliage dramatically increases visibility from the path below the ledges. Walkers should be reminded that because deer, bear, and moose are well established in the densely wooded range around the mountain, this is an active area during hunting season, so it is wisest to plan your walk for another time.

28. Schoodic Head/
Winter Harbor

A pretty, low summit composed of the pink, granodioritic rock common to the Mount Desert region, Schoodic Head provides excellent views of the waters off the Schoodic Peninsula and across Frenchman Bay to the west. It lies in the mainland portion of Acadia National Park, which occupies the southwestern side of the Schoodic Peninsula below the towns of Winter Harbor and Birch Harbor. The coastline here is composed of dozens of beautiful tidal inlets lined with picturesque, dense coniferous woodlands. It is the sort of Maine terrain that tends to wind up on magazine covers and in scenic calendars.

To hike Schoodic Head, drive south from U.S. Route 1 on Maine Route 186 from West Gouldsboro. Follow the signs to Winter Harbor. There are some good outlooks west toward Flanders Bay and Frenchman Bay as you continue south. In Winter Harbor, keep left following Maine Route 186 to the Park Service Road, about two-thirds of a mile east of the village center. Turn south and right at the park entrance and drive toward Schoodic Point. Shortly you cross an inlet and pass Frazer Point. The road then runs down the east side of Frenchman Bay, with dramatic views across to Mount Desert Island. Passing West Pond, the road shortly arrives at a junction. Keep left here, continuing around the point. Watch carefully for the Blueberry Hill turnout on your right. (All traffic in this section is one-way; if you miss the trailhead, you'll have to make the complete loop around the point before you'll get to the spot you're looking for.) Park at the Blueberry Hill turnout.

The trail up Schoodic Head leaves the left (north) side of the road just before the entrance to the parking lot. A small, weathered sign marks the trailhead. Take the trail northwest up the remains of a grassy road through a corridor of smooth alder. You soon crest the rise and walk through stands of red and white spruce, passing ledge outcrops on both sides of the path. Going by a white paper birch whose limbs are growing at right angles, you proceed farther

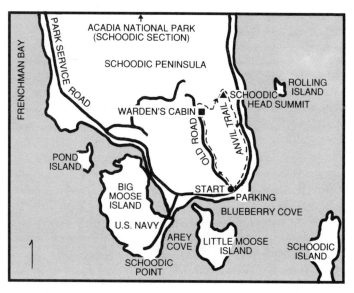

north, rising again. Another alder swamp appears on your left, and you walk north through two wet and boggy depressions. Northern white cedar grows off the path. After running over level ground, the route climbs slightly again through more alders and a birch grove by a little pond. Over this hump, the trail runs past the warden's cabin, where you *continue straight ahead* on the gravel road. A few yards past the cabin, you come to the Schoodic Head Trail, which runs east up the mountain. It's just under a mile from here to the summit.

Walking eastward now, you climb briskly through a cluster of boulders in groves of spruce and hemlock. This forest thrives on the moist air that continually rises from the ocean. Haircap moss and various shelf fungi cling to rocks and decaying logs. Climbing more steeply through an area of blow-downs, the red-blazed trail soon reaches a series of exposed ledges on the left. You pull around to the north and climb to a plateau briefly, then rise more steeply again up through the right-hand side of a cleft in the ledge. The trail then rises farther through more exposed rock and ledge, crossing a small brook.

Now the trail begins to deliver some of the views for which it is famous. Emerging into the open on ledges dotted with jack-pine scrub, you can look west here to the islands of Frenchman Bay and the major peaks of Mount Desert. On a clear day, this is probably the finest view of Acadia anywhere. Walk over more ledges to the east, dropping through a sheltered depression. The trail winds through clutches of rhodora and emerges on the east summit ledges in a few minutes. Here, splendid views over Schoodic and Wonsqueak harbors open up. Islands are visible immediately offshore, and on an exceptionally clear day,

you may see the islands of Petit Manan far to the east.

When you're ready to leave this pretty spot, you may either return to the road on the route you followed coming up or take the Anvil Trail, which runs southeastward to the road. Dropping through scattered groves of jack pines with their distinctive, weathered gray cones, the trail runs down through loose scree. Sheep laurel, ground juniper, and spruce line the trail as you descend to a notch known as the Anvil. Below here, the trail continues to the east and south through red-spruce groves. Patches of reindeer and antler lichens are seen in the groundcover. The trail reaches the road in about a mile from the summit. Turn *right* on the paved road and walk west to your car just a short distance away.

The round trip to Schoodic Head via the warden's cabin both ways is about 3⅔ miles and requires a leisurely 2½ hours of walking. The loop route, climbing via the warden's cabin and descending over the Anvil, covers about 2¾ miles and takes roughly two hours. The ground is rough in sections of both the Schoodic Head Trail and the Anvil Trail, so hikers should wear appropriate boots.

Once off the mountain, to regain U.S. Route 1, drive north on the park road up the west side of Schoodic Harbor, past Wonsqueak and Bunker harbors to the junction with Maine Route 186 in Birch Harbor. Bear left on Route 186 and follow it through Winter Harbor west and north to Route 1.

29. GREAT WASS ISLAND PRESERVE/BEALS

Great Wass Island juts out into the Atlantic farther than any other mainland-connected terrain between Schoodic Head and the Canadian border. Part of the town of Beals, Great Wass is home to a Nature Conservancy preserve of more than fifteen hundred acres, through which run two interesting trails that culminate in walks along the pounding, open Atlantic. Great Wass Island Preserve provides sanctuary to many important bird and animal species. On its ocean side, below Eastern Bay, Great Wass offers excellent opportunities to observe marine life, particularly the seals that frequent the ledges here. Although close to settled fishing communities in Beals and Jonesport, the Great Wass Preserve is a wild area of great natural beauty, and a superb place to walk the coast away

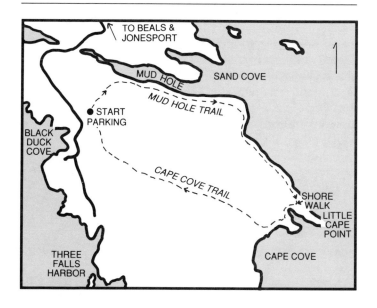

from the mainland crowds.

From U.S. Route 1 just north of Columbia Falls, turn south on Maine Route 187 and drive southeast to Jonesport via Indian River. The scattered houses often show the paraphernalia of lobstering, fishing, or logging— all traditional local occupations. The road follows the high ridge of the Addison-Jonesport peninsula, dropping down to the sea at Jonesport, one of few Maine communities still dedicated largely to taking a living from the sea.

From Jonesport, you cross the bridge over Moosabec Reach to Beals and continue south, watching for a fork in the road where the *right-hand* turn is marked by a "nature preserve" sign. This road shortly becomes gravel as it winds southward past a number of open inlets. As you descend around a bend, Black Duck Cove is on your right, and opposite it on your left are the trailhead and parking area, marked by a large signboard and trail register.

After signing in at the register, the walker has a choice of two hikes across Great Wass to its rocky Atlantic side. The more northerly route, the Mud Hole Trail, runs northeast and east along an inlet known as the Mud Hole. Passing through white-birch groves and mixed coniferous forest, the trail reaches the shoreline south of Sand Cove and above Little Cape Point. Hikers can walk along the shore around the point and return on the other trail from Cape Cove to the south, or they can simply retrace their original route.

The slightly longer path, the Cape Cove Trail, runs right and southeast just beyond the trailhead. This route traverses fairly level ground through thick, mossy spruce forests. It also takes you through several heath-like bogs and a swampy area grown up with sundew and pitcher plant in season. Jack pines flourish in the ledgy, open spots. Roseroot sedum, Hooker's iris, and Laurentian primrose grow among the rocks. Plenty of opportunities for shoreline exploration exist here, and you may observe seals on ledges to the southeast.

Whichever route you walk, you'll find Great Wass a quiet haven for osprey, spruce grouse, and black-capped and boreal chickadees. A wide variety of shore-birds can be seen, and the endangered bald eagle visits from nesting sites on nearby islands. Great blue herons feed in the protected inlets.

The Maine Chapter of The Nature Conservancy, in its indispensable book, *Maine Forever,* reports that Great Wass Island's vegetation is more typical of ter-rain farther north. Trees such as the jack pine, which is more likely to be found significantly to the north or in alpine zones, prosper here in the cold, wet ocean winds, clinging to the acidic, rocky soil. The heathlike areas are similarly unusual, being more typical of the Canadian Maritimes. Great Wass is the limit of their range.

Given the fragile and unique quality of the island's plant and animal life, visitors should use care in walk-ing and should remove no flowers, groundcover, or shrubs. As with any walk that includes sections di-rectly on shore rocks and ledges, both trails on Great Wass should be used with caution. Though it is pos-sible to walk directly on the tidal shoreline at the end of both the trails mentioned here, walkers must use caution on slippery ledges and rocks that are often overgrown with seaweed. Keep well above the waterline at high tide and during ocean storms; there is a strong undertow, and rescue would be doubtful.

From the parking area, a round trip via either the Mud Hole Trail or the Cape Cove Trail takes between two and two-and-a-half hours. Additional time should be budgeted for exploring the shoreline and for making a loop by starting on the Mud Hole Trail and returning via the Cape Cove Trail. Walkers should also be aware that hunters pursue white-tailed deer within the pre-serve. If you walk here during deer-hunting season, wear plenty of red and fluorescent orange.

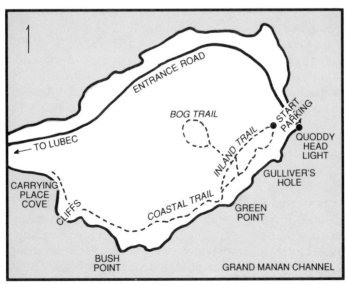

1

ENTRANCE ROAD

BOG TRAIL

START
PARKING

TO LUBEC

INLAND TRAIL

QUODDY
HEAD
LIGHT

GULLIVER'S
HOLE

CARRYING
PLACE
COVE

CLIFFS

COASTAL TRAIL

GREEN
POINT

BUSH
POINT

GRAND MANAN CHANNEL

30. QUODDY HEAD STATE PARK/LUBEC

A rounded peninsula of land on the Grand Manan Channel, Quoddy Head hovers like a sea-wracked, brooding sentinel over the waters of the cold North Atlantic at the easternmost point of the United States. The west and northwest sides of the peninsula are marsh or open, rolling meadow fronting on Lubec. The east and southeast perimeter of Quoddy is less gentle. Great cliffs plunge to the sea, and twenty-foot tides are the rule here. West Quoddy Head Light, one of Maine's most prominent coastal warning beacons, sits dramatically perched on the outer border of the land, its presence a constant reminder to haul clear of this rocky place. Across the channel, Grand Manan hangs in the mist.

Quoddy Head possesses the much-photographed cold, hard beauty of the northern Maine coast. This is also an ecologically rich and absorbing place to explore on foot. Luckily, most of the land on the seaward side of the head is now a state park open for day use; it is a sublime location for walking directly through the natural world of this rugged chunk of coastline.

Quoddy Head State Park is reached by turning east off U.S. Route 1 opposite the Whiting Community Church in Whiting and driving east toward Lubec on Maine Route 189. Just before you come to Lubec proper, watch for a turn on the right ten miles from Route 1. A large sign marks the turn toward Quoddy Head. This side road winds south and east toward the peninsula, with occasional views across the bay to Lubec. Four-and-three-quarter miles from Route 189, you come to the park entrance and the lighthouse.

Drive right and park in the state lot.

At the front of the parking area, several display signs will give you an idea of where you can walk on the park's three main trails. First, try a visit to West Quoddy Head Light. This path leaves the northeast corner of the parking area and winds down to the lighthouse in just a few hundred yards. The grounds of this distinctive striped tower are open to walkers. The lighthouse itself is now an automated facility, its last caretaker departing several years ago to loud local protest. (Only a tiny minority of the lighthouses on the United States coast are still actively staffed by full-time personnel. The United States Coast Guard, which has been performing heroically for generations while undermanned and underfunded, has had to automate more and more of the beacons. Fishermen and commercial pilots have opposed the move to automation, as they know that automated devices fail, sometimes at very dangerous moments. In a mean chop and thick fog, a lighthouse beacon gone dark because of "technical difficulties" would leave even experienced sailors in a nasty situation as they tried to negotiate this tricky channel. It is a strange government policy that says we can afford thousand-dollar wrenches but cannot afford to staff the lifesaving lighthouses of our coasts.)

Returning to the parking lot, you will find three other interesting trails that, together, offer a full day's walking about various corners of the head. These walks are noted on one of the display panels mentioned earlier. The longest route is the Coastal Trail, which makes a four-mile round trip around the southeast perimeter of the head to Carrying Place Cove and back. This trail stays closest to the waterline and provides dramatic views of the rocky headland, running past Gulliver's Hole, Green Point, and Bush Point. The round trip can be done in a comfortable two hours, though you will probably want to add another hour for exploration and picture taking.

The Inland Trail takes you through the inner precincts of Quoddy Head, providing an opportunity to examine the attractive, densely grown coniferous forest common to this section of the Maine coast. The Inland Trail eventually winds its way southwestward to the ocean at Green Point. You may retrace your steps from there or pick up the Coastal Trail and follow it northeastward back to the parking area. Either way, the Inland Trail provides a two-mile round trip and takes a bit over an hour.

The Bog Trail makes a loop around a swampy lowland in the middle of the preserve. This is an appealing walk for birders and those interested in wildlife. The Bog Trail lies off the Inland Trail, about three-quarters of a mile west of the parking area.

If you wish to combine these paths into a long, continuous walk that will take up most of a glorious day, try this: On the outbound leg, walk the full length of the Coastal Trail to Carrying Place Cove, enjoying the marvelous ocean views. After lunch, walk back along the Coastal Trail to Green Point, turning left on the Inland Trail. When you reach the Bog Trail, turn onto it to the northwest. Emerging from the Bog Trail loop, return to the Inland Trail and continue northeastward to your car.

Remember that the park is open for day use only and that the gates close at dusk.

31. Cobscook Bay State Park/ Edmunds

Cobscook Bay State Park nestles on the western side of Cobscook Bay opposite Eastport in the middle of the attractive arc of coastline between Pembroke and Whiting. The park consists of nearly nine hundred acres of woodlands right on the edge of a bay characterized by the Indians as a place of "boiling tides." Indeed, tides here run twenty-four to twenty-eight feet along a shore notable for its exceptional beauty. For those who want not only to walk the Maine coast but also to picnic or camp on its shores, the park offers fine camping and picnicking facilities. This spot makes an excellent base for exploring other nearby walking areas, including Quoddy Head, Fort O'Brien State Park in Machiasport, and Campobello Island in New Brunswick. Moosehorn National Wildlife Refuge in Calais and Baring (also described in this book) is just a short drive away. The park is open for camping from mid-May to mid-October, but hikers are welcome in the off-season, too. Just leave your car outside the gate and walk in.

The park entrance is on the Lower Edmunds Road in the Edmunds section of Dennysville. Watch for signs six miles south of Dennysville center on U.S. Route 1. Turn east off Route 1 at the park signs and drive for about a half-mile. The park gate is on the right. Just inside the gate is the registration building. Park here well to the right. A guide to birds seen in the park and a small natural history library are available for visitor use at the registration building. A small fee is charged for entry in summer.

From the registration area, walk west and northwest on the marked nature trail. This route arches around to the south and southeast through attractive stands of spruce and fir in a heavily wooded section of the park. You soon come to the inner reaches of Burnt Cove, where there are opportunities for exploring the shoreline when the tide is out. The trail gradually loops around to the southeast, the blue-blazed route bringing you out on a park road that you follow southwest to a headland between Burnt Cove and Broad Cove. Bear right here and continue the length of the road to a picnic area on the lip of the bay. There are excellent water views here on three sides, and this is a grand place for day visitors to enjoy their lunch.

From this neck of land, retrace your steps to the point where you emerged from the nature trail. Just past a spring, bear right on another road and follow this along Broad Cove until you come to the main entrance road. Bear right and southeast here, following the signs to the boat launching ramp northeast of Whiting Bay. The bay runs up on a layer of shingle here, and on a good day, kayakers and powerboaters

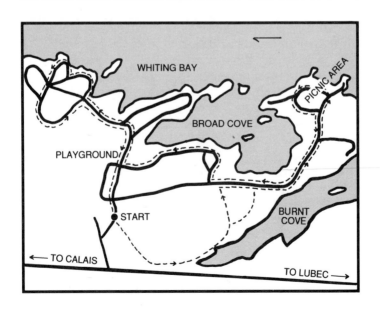

use the ramp as they head out for a run on the beautiful, island-studded waters.

Stay on the park road as it dips past a pond, following the shore in a loop to the northeast. As the road bears left and around to the north, you will see a fire tower not far away. It can be climbed (at your own risk) for excellent outlooks along the coastal area. The tower is manned periodically during the summer, depending upon fire danger. Returning to the loop, retrace your steps past the boat ramp, and then, slowly bearing around to the right, follow the main road uphill and back to the entrance lot and your car. Total distance for this walk is about 1¼ miles.

As with all Maine state parks with overnight accommodations, places at Cobscook Bay can be reserved after January 1 of each year on a first-come, first-served basis. The park has spaces for both tenters and mobile campers in separate areas. Write Cobscook Bay State Park, P.O. Box 51, Dennysville, ME 04628.

32. MOOSEHORN NATIONAL WILDLIFE REFUGE/BARING

Washington County forms the easternmost corner of Maine— a portion of the state that remains largely undeveloped, rustically attractive, and unspoiled. If you look at a map, you'll note that, except for the coastal settlements and a handful of inland crossroads towns, the county belongs to lakes, mountains, and lonely back-country. Snugged up against the Canadian border, Moosehorn National Wildlife Refuge is a natural preserve of nearly sixteen hundred acres that came under federal protection as a link in the Atlantic Flyway in 1937. The refuge contains a variety of terrain, from dense coniferous

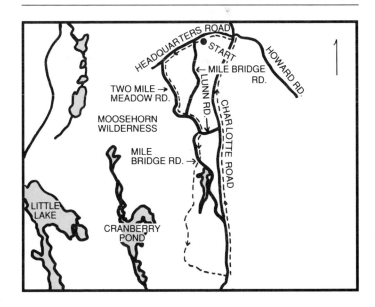

woods to open marsh; several lakes and brooks; and the kind of grassy upland that is highly attractive to migrating birds. Moosehorn is quintessential Washington County.

Close to 220 bird species have been sighted here. Large rare species, such as the American bald eagle and peregrine falcon, nest within this range. Cooper's hawks, turkey vultures, rough-legged hawks, and American kestrels are seen. Great horned and barred owls are common. Twenty-six species of geese and ducks have been sighted, and both the great blue and green-backed herons are waders in the refuge. In short, for anyone interested in observing an amazing mix of important bird types, Moosehorn provides a rare setting in which to walk and observe.

Because the lands within Moosehorn are so varied, ideal habitats exist for a wide range of mammalian species. Spruce, balsam, and deciduous second-growth forest provide cover for woodland and meadow jumping mice, moles, shrews, chipmunks, red and gray squirrels, snowshoe hare, woodchuck, beaver, muskrat, porcupine, and raccoon. Fisher, mink, shorttail weasel, river otter, longtail weasel, and striped skunk are also residents of the refuge. White-tailed deer, moose, and black bear are game species in Moosehorn. *Canis latrans,* the redoubtable coyote, is common in the high ground of the preserve.

Moosehorn is reached by going west from Calais on U.S. Route 1 for about $3\frac{1}{2}$ miles, watching for Charlotte Road on your left. Turn south on Charlotte Road as it parallels the Magurrewock Marsh to the left (east). The Magurrewock leads to Goodall Heath and a chain of ponds, all of which add up to first-class migratory bird ground. Driving south here, particularly in spring and fall, you're likely to see a lot of waterfowl activity in the pockets of marsh to your left.

Two-and-a-half miles south of Route 1, the gravel road into refuge headquarters leaves Charlotte Road to the right. Parking is available around the headquarters buildings. An interpretive board provides information on the refuge, and maps of the refuge grounds can be obtained here, too.

Moosehorn, big as it is, does not have a very extensive trail network, but plenty of excellent walking is available on some of the old woods roads that border the eastern edge of the Moosehorn wilderness, a large, rough tract of land on the northwest side of the refuge. For those who do not want to trek too far back into the brush, a short self-guiding nature trail has been created in the vicinity of the headquarters buildings. This trail departs to the left off the gravel road just beyond and behind the warden's house. Pamphlets describing the route are usually available in a box by the trailhead.

More adventurous walkers can make a long loop along the east side of the wilderness, around Mile Bridge Flowage and Sunken Bog, out to Charlotte Road, and then north to headquarters again through prime woodcock country. This loop may be of varying lengths: four, six, or eight miles, depending on how much energy you've got. Leaving your car at headquarters, walk west on the gravel road for about a mile. You'll pass Mile Bridge Road on your left shortly after leaving the built-up area. Reach Two Mile Meadow Road on your left, a little under a mile from the headquarters field. Bear left on Two Mile Meadow Road and walk south now through Otter Flowage and Maccrae Flowage. These two waterways are likely places for observing both bird and animal life. You join Mile Bridge Road, which comes in on the left, in another mile.

If you want to hold this walk to about four-and-a-half miles, watch for Lunn Road, coming up shortly on your left. You can follow this road left and east to Charlotte Road, then turn north on the paved surface to return to the headquarters. If you want a longer, more remote walk, simply continue south on Mile Bridge Road and watch for a grassy tote road on your right in about three-quarters of a mile. If you stay on the main road here, you'll pass through Mile Bridge Flowage and come out on Charlotte Road in another

mile. From there, you walk northward to the headquarters road. If you keep right here instead and go
down wooded Youngs Road, you will walk southwest
along the periphery of the wilderness, coming, in less
than two miles, to a junction with Cranberry Outlet
Road. Keep *left* at that junction, gradually working
your way around to the east, with Cranberry Brook in
the brush to your right. Going eastward, you arrive
shortly at the paved Charlotte Road. Go north, as
with the other return options, to headquarters.

Whether you go the full distance on this route or
take a shorter return, the walk back along Charlotte
Road can be done on the road proper or on the old
Maine Central Railroad roadbed that parallels it. Both
the road and the railbed pass through grassy swale
and scrub that is prime habitat for American woodcock. Many bird fanciers visit Moosehorn just to
watch the fascinating mating ritual of this species.
The mating season is from mid-April to about the end
of the first week in May each year. The shy birds are
best observed in the hour before sunrise and for
about an hour around sunset. The refuge is one of
the few places in eastern America where woodcock
are found in such abundance.

Walkers in the back-country of the Moosehorn
Refuge should be aware that the term *road* means
anything from a graded gravel surface suitable for
most vehicles, to a grassy, brushy right-of-way that is
not much more than two tracks through the woods.
Road markings are few or nonexistent. The ground is
rough and wild if you're off the roads. The best walking is probably in spring and fall, when the hungry
insects of high summer aren't around. Hunting is
allowed in most sections of the refuge, so walk only in
"No Hunting" areas when hunters are in the woods.

For further enquiries, send a stamped, self-
addressed envelope to: Refuge Manager, Moosehorn
National Wildlife Refuge, P.O. Box 1077, Calais, ME
04619.